THE A–Z OF SPECIAL EDUCATIONAL NEEDS

NEIL MASLEN & LINDSAY COOPER-SMITH

SERIES EDITOR: ROY BLATCHFORD

JOHN CATT
FROM HODDER EDUCATION

To order, please visit www.johncatt.com or contact Customer Service at education@hachette.co.uk / +44 (0)1235 827827.

ISBN: 978 1 0360 0495 8

© Neil Maslen and Lindsay Cooper-Smith 2024

First published in 2024 by
John Catt from Hodder Education,
An Hachette UK Company
15 Riduna Park, Station Road,
Melton, Woodbridge IP12 1QT
www.johncatt.com

The authorised representative in the EEA is Hachette Ireland, 8 Castlecourt Centre, Dublin 15, D15 XTP3, Ireland (email: info@hbgi.ie)

Photograph on page 125 © Shutterstock/Monkey Business Images

Typeset in the UK.

Printed in the UK.

A catalogue record for this title is available from the British Library.

ABOUT THE AUTHORS

Neil Maslen is the Director of Education for Speech and Language UK, a charity that focuses on helping children with speech and language challenges (https://speechandlanguage.org.uk/). With a diverse leadership background, Neil has thrived in various roles, from head of college in a large London secondary school to SENCo and headteacher in the south-west of England. He applied this experience in his previous role as education and standards manager at a large multi-academy trust, where he empowered and guided headteachers across primary and secondary schools to drive school improvement. Neil's passion lies in supporting vulnerable children and nurturing the development of staff, helping them reach their full potential as teachers, leaders and SENCos.

Lindsay Cooper-Smith is the Director of Inclusion for a large primary multi-academy trust in the south-west of England and has a real passion for inclusion that drives her to champion every child. She has worked in a variety of schools across the city of Plymouth and has always been drawn to supporting the most vulnerable children. As a SENCo, she loved to work with families and collaborate with other agencies to maximise impact. Lindsay helped to develop a provision to support primary-aged children at risk of exclusion within the city. This provision grew to offer outreach and forest school and was recommended and partially funded by the local authority.

CONTENTS

Section Two

Resources for professional development:

FOREWORD

A quarter way through the twenty-first century, we stand at a crossroads in English education with regard to children with special educational needs and disabilities (SEND).

As the authors wisely remind us in their excellent *History* chapter, the Warnock Report of 1978 and the Education Act of 1981 marked vital step-changes in our schooling system. Thereafter, children and young people with special educational needs could have proper access to classroom learning, with appropriate support.

Yet take these statistics from one of the largest local authorities in the country: in 2016, the county was responsible for 7550 children with an Education, Health and Care Plan (EHCP). In January 2024, the number increased to 13,228. And with only a gently expanding overall school population, the county has seen an irresistible rise in the number of EHCPs; an increase of 28% since March 2021.

It is this demand – and its inevitable cost – that places our education system at a crossroads.

There is no financial cavalry on the horizon. School leaders are going to have to find positive solutions to meet the needs of the vast majority of children *within* mainstream schools. The nation's special schools are in good heart but there is simply not the capacity within them to address the burgeoning numbers of youngsters who have identified special needs.

Against this backcloth, *The A–Z of Special Educational Needs* is an unashamed celebration of the importance of leading special educational needs in primary and secondary schools, rooted in the authors' experiences and extensive research with SEND leaders. The book captures the joys and rewards as well as some of the frustrations and challenges.

It is, in part, an honest account of what being a Special Educational Needs Co-ordinator (SENCo) is like: see especially pages 159–166. We hope the content may inspire you to become one in your school or, if you are already practising the art, guide you into becoming an even better one. As a handbook of tried-and-tested practice, it has been designed to be dipped in and out of as the need demands.

A SENCo occupies a unique position in a school. In common with the headteacher, there is usually only one of you but, unlike the headteacher, the SENCo *requires* an additional qualification to undertake the role. This should demonstrate to everyone in education – parents, the local authority, as well as other stakeholders – the importance of this position in the school.

Neil Maslen and Lindsay Cooper-Smith have both served as SENCos and worked with many leaders of special needs in schools and across multi-academy trusts. Their authoritative narrative demonstrates how much they truly value colleagues' tenacity and determination to support some of our most educationally vulnerable children.

The authors make very clear that the role is not for the faint hearted as they take the reader on an informative journey from **Adaptive** and **Disability**, through **EHCP** and **IEP**, to **Yearning** and **Zones**. In the words of Theodore Roosevelt, 'nothing worth having comes easy'.

Note: In this A–Z title, the term SEND (Special Educational Needs and Disabilities) is used to encompass the range of learning difficulties or disabilities that can hinder a child or young person's learning compared to their peers.

Roy Blatchford, series editor

SECTION ONE

ADAPTIVE

In order to succeed as a leader of special educational needs, you need to be able to adapt and respond in an agile manner.

The education system is always changing and you may need to adapt to these changes and support others to adapt. There are two elements to this chapter: how to adapt in your role, but also how teachers could and should use an adaptive teaching approach in their lessons and how you can valuably assist them.

Being adaptive is not just about what happens in the classroom, but also describes the very role of a SENCo. There are not many positions in a school that have to deal with so many different stakeholders, often at the same time or in very close succession. These interactions may not be planned, making that process of adapting to different scenarios all the more challenging.

Let's paint a picture of what a typical day might look like.

You arrive at school and meet with a teacher who is struggling to manage a pupil in their class and does not feel they are meeting their needs. They are visibly anxious and upset, so not only need some practical advice, but also some gentle reassurance. As you finish with this, you get a call from the school office telling you a parent has arrived at reception asking to see you. You know what this is about and, although you have a meeting with the local authority (LA) that you need to plan for, you know that dealing with this now will make things easier in the long term.

This is then followed by a staff briefing, then the pre-arranged meeting. Later that day you need to deal with a behaviour issue at break, and observe and feed back to a teacher on an aspect of their teaching. After that, you have a meeting with the headteacher about a governing body meeting that evening at which you are presenting some data. So, a little extreme, perhaps, but let's list all the people who required a level of interaction (with the SENCo providing a high level of information) often with little preparation:

1. Teacher requiring emotional and practical support for them to manage their day effectively
2. Challenging parent arriving at reception demanding information and support
3. Staff briefing – taking in information on the school day
4. LA meeting about an individual pupil, requiring in-depth knowledge of a child so that additional funding can be obtained
5. A planned lesson visit and feedback to a teacher on how to support a pupil with a specific learning need that needed some prior research
6. Meeting with the headteacher
7. Presentation of data to the governing body.

This variety is what makes the role so appealing to some and so enjoyable for others. Your preparation and leadership will be key in order to help you manage this.

As a lead for special needs in your school, you will need to be up to date with current research, publications and advice and this will support you in your many roles. You should also be aware of what is available within your trust, or local SENCo network, as well as the local authority, to support children with SEN. It is helpful to be part of email groups to receive notifications of current initiatives that might be available, including funding. Two very useful organisations are the Education Endowment Foundation (EEF) and the National Association for Special Educational Needs (NASEN). Where possible, you should request from the school leadership team to attend local authority SENCo briefings or similar.

Being part of local area or organisations' working parties and task and finish groups can give SENCos a good knowledge of what may be available but also allows them to share their expertise on what schools and children need, helping to shape the local offer and landscape for identified children and their families.

ADAPTIVE TEACHING

There has been a shift in professional vocabulary from 'differentiation' to 'adaptive teaching'. What does that mean and why is the change necessary?

In a blog for the EEF, Jon Eaton (2022) states that adaptive teaching is about 'being responsive to information about learning, then adjusting teaching to better match pupil need'. It involves teaching the same lesson objectives to all pupils while providing scaffolds (a metaphor for support that is removed in response to a pupil's need) to allow all pupils to make progress. Rather than planning different activities for different groups depending on attainment levels, adaptive teaching is adapting whole-class teaching so everyone can access the learning objective.

This is not new. It is part of the Teachers' Standards (2011) that staff 'will adapt teaching to respond to the strengths and needs of all pupils'. Adaptive teaching is also referenced in Standard 5 of the UK Government's Early career framework (2019). Early career teachers (ECTs) are recommended to work with the special needs leader and show an understanding of the SEND Code of Practice (2014) in regards to this standard.

The shift has occurred as there is a risk that when differentiating, expectations may be lowered which can create 'ceilings' for pupils, particularly those who may have SEND or be lower attaining. Sometimes this tenuous link between activity and teacher input can lead to disengagement by our pupils with SEND. Florian and Black-Hawkins (2013) believe that inclusion is more effective when teachers focus on what is to be taught, rather than who is to learn.

Often when differentiating, teachers would be creating several mini lessons within a lesson. Therefore, in principle, when teachers are adapting rather than differentiating, their workload should be less. Differentiation can sometimes exclude pupils from whole-class opportunities and allow for 'coasting'. Thus, instead of identifying reasons for difference, we need to respond to individual differences.

As teachers, we all know that pupils learn at different rates and require different levels and types of support at different points in their education in order to succeed. Assessment allows teachers to ascertain what children know, what their barriers might be and what they need to learn next. Adapting teaching in a responsive way to this knowledge by providing targeted support to pupils who are struggling is likely to increase pupil success.

Differentiation is considered still valid and appropriate when a child is working significantly below their peers by, say, two years or more.

Examples of adaptive teaching

Barriers to learning can include vocabulary, behaviour, production skills (such as writing), ability to decode, and a limited working memory. Teachers should be supported by the SENCo to think of methods to adapt their teaching to remove these barriers or provide targeted support to develop skills that may be causing barriers.

Here is a particular example of adaptive teaching linked to resources. If teaching a science lesson where pupils are asked to research the parts of a plant, teachers may want to provide reading texts that are at an appropriate reading level to particular groups of pupils. There may be opportunity for pre-teaching, where the child can read a text in advance of the lesson or can be supported in understanding the text by an adult prior to the lesson. The activity could be scaffolded to provide pupils with support to achieve the objective and task. This could be the use of a writing frame or an opportunity to cut and stick rather than write.

Pupils may need learning to be given a context or linked to previous learning or events. Pictures or videos could be used to do this prior to the lesson. Specific vocabulary linked to topics may need to be taught beforehand to allow pupils to access the teacher input fully.

Adaptive teaching may also be linked to behaviour. Pupils should be provided with opportunities to learn and develop appropriate behaviour for learning through intervention or adult support.

Pupils with sensory needs or hearing/visual impairments may need to have the accessibility of resources considered. Is the font big enough? Where are they seated in the classroom?

By using assessment for learning, teachers are able to provide adaptations in the moment; this may be as simple as changing their language or clarifying next steps. It may also be providing examples of completed tasks. Peer support can not only allow pupils to extend and consolidate their learning by explaining to a peer, it can also support those pupils who are not yet confident by having it explained by a fellow pupil in a different way. Sometimes it may be appropriate to set some learners to work individually while a few who need further explanation attempt the activity as a group before moving on to work independently.

Adaptive teaching is for all. If a pupil needs adaptations made in order to succeed, it does not automatically mean they should be on the SEND register and considered for SEND Support.

However, if a pupil needs targeted/intervention-style support for a prolonged period (longer than six weeks), this provision would be considered 'additional to and different from their peers' and would result in the child warranting an Individualised Education Plan (IEP) and being added to the SEND register. These decisions should be made in collaboration with the SENCo, who would ultimately make the decision. Targeted interventions can be measured using the 'assess, plan, do, review' cycle to ensure it is what the child needs. This provision should be shared with parents and reviewed regularly.

Whether adapting learning to support all pupils to learn or adapting your own practice to ensure your interactions across the day are managed appropriately, it is vital for a SENCo to understand and be reflective in their role in order to succeed.

ASIDE

What is the purpose of adaptive teaching?

When thinking about adaptive teaching, what is the priority?

- Is it for all children to reach the same outcome?
- Is it for children to develop their independence through scaffolding?
- Is it to encourage an equity of education?
- Is it to allow all children to experience success?

BEHAVIOUR

Probably one of the biggest challenges for a leader of special needs is the behaviour of children and young people, and the impact that can have on others socially, on the learning of all, and on the general wellbeing of a school.

Everyone wants all the answers and everyone wants them yesterday and, quite often, the first port of call for solutions is the SENCo. However, behaviour is complex and for some pupils, even the most comprehensive and consistent behaviour policy may not support them in a mainstream school. It is not your sole responsibility to support and develop this – everyone has a role in this throughout the school. All teachers value how effectively a school creates a safe, calm, orderly and positive environment, and the impact this has on pupil behaviour and attitudes; this cannot be the remit or responsibility of just one person.

Managing behaviour in schools is a particularly controversial topic, with many people advocating a rigid approach – often referred to as 'zero tolerance' by its critics – rather than a more trauma-informed approach, based on relational and restorative practice, which some feel is the cause of, or can increase, poor behaviour. In reality, the most effective approach is somewhere in the middle; as with many of the more controversial elements to education, it is very rarely binary.

It is important that there is a policy based in research and experience. Arguably, Paul Dix, through the work in his 2017 book *When the Adults Change, Everything Changes*, has had a really significant impact on schools' behaviour policies in the last few years, minimising the number of school rules and ensuring restorative practice is part of any sanction, if sanctions are even necessary. As SENCo, and as with all policies, you need to have the opportunity to review behaviour policies and provide input with the views of a pupil with SEND. Is the policy written with some of the most vulnerable pupils in mind? Would it meet the equalities duty for some of these children? How would it impact on them?

All stakeholders need to be part of the design and implementation of a behaviour policy. They all need to buy in and understand what will happen and why. The policy should include the outcome if a pupil does or does not follow the school rules. Some schools believe that rewards are not essential and that intrinsic rewards are the most impactful. Others may use certificates, recognition boards, phone calls home or physical prizes for good behaviour.

If pupils begin to show negative behaviour, warnings are often used. This can be verbal or, sometimes, visual. Some schools use behaviour charts/displays where pupils' names are moved as a precursor/warning before they receive a sanction. Often at primary school, symbols such as traffic lights, rain clouds or cakes may be used as a visual representation of where a child is in relation to a reward or sanction. If behaviour charts/displays are used, it is important that these are not designed to shame pupils but to encourage positive behaviour. If a pupil's name has been moved in relation to a negative action, the adult should be looking to move the name back as quickly as possible to avoid shaming.

As a leader of special needs, what influence should you have in this sort of approach? Should there, or even can there, be differences for different pupils?

With regards to sanctions, some schools have zero tolerance if children are not following the school rules or for certain non-negotiable behaviours, such as physical behaviour or vaping. These sanctions can include missed break/play times, internal seclusion, suspension and, finally, exclusion. Other schools, particularly those following a trauma-informed approach, may use natural consequences with restorative conversations. An example of this would be a child putting up a display they had ripped down in a moment of dysregulation.

The policy also needs to consider how behaviour will be measured and shared with parents. Most schools, if not all, use online recording systems such as BehaviourWatch or CPOMS. These allow schools to measure the impact of their policy on behaviour in the school. In recording and measuring incidents of negative behaviour, the senior leadership team can analyse when incidents are happening and what the triggers for these incidents are.

It is important for the SENCo to analyse the behaviour of the pupils on the SEND register for several reasons. Most importantly, it is to look at who is causing the highest number of incidents as they are likely not learning in lessons and will be causing some disruption to others. Such pupils are demonstrating that they need additional support whether that be academically or with their social, emotional or mental-health needs. This information can also be used to direct intervention for children or conversations with parents.

Reviewing which teachers are recording the most incidents may show that an individual teacher or a group of teachers need some support. This could be through additional professional development; alternatively, different deployment of a teaching assistant could be part of the solution.

If there is a teacher who appears to be struggling more with managing behaviour, it would be appropriate to put support in place. However, fewer behaviour logs may not always mean that the teacher is managing behaviour well.

If there is an area of the school that seems to be a place for regular incidents of negative behaviour, it would make sense to place more staff in this area or review the environment.

Despite significant support and interventions, some pupils in schools will ultimately be excluded. A significant majority of these children are on the SEND register and will have EHCPs. As the SENCo, you may be asked to attend or provide evidence for a disciplinary panel for an excluded pupil. The authors have sat on and chaired many disciplinary panels and been faced with an endless list of behaviour incidents. It is important to see what additional support/interventions were put in place for a particular pupil and how the school made any reasonable adaptations to their provision. If it is clear this has happened effectively, it provides a much stronger argument for governance to uphold the school's decision, ensuring the school is abiding by the Equality Act (2010) to create the appropriate provision for children with SEND.

There will always be pupils who sit outside of the behaviour policy for a number of reasons. However, all of these could fit under the remit of the SENCo. Some of the reasons are detailed here:

Provision: is the provision appropriate to enable the pupil to adhere to the school rules? Lessons need to be adapted to meet the pupil's needs. Does the pupil need pre-teaching in order to engage in the lesson? Is the task achievable? Can the pupil succeed?

Environment: is the environment distracting or conducive to learning? Pupils with sensory needs may find even the calmest of classrooms challenging. There may be a need for:

- regular breaks – brain breaks/physical breaks
- modifications to the environment – removal of busy/cluttered displays; addition of work stations or dividers
- additional resources. Resources such as fiddle toys can support individuals in the classroom. Ear defenders, weighted blankets or tension bands may also support a pupil to remain focused.

Environment can also refer to a pupil's home environment and past/present trauma or adverse childhood experiences. Behaviour is often described as a communication of unmet need. The SENCo can facilitate a team to lead positive change for the family. For example, while in school, providing opportunity for therapeutic and talk interventions. In some cases, the school may need to take advice from a representative from Social Care, however this should always be managed carefully and collaboratively with parents.

There are things the school can implement to support pupils who arrive at school not in a place to be 'ready to learn'. Maslow's hierarchy of needs (1943) is clear that children are not able to learn if their basic needs are not being met. Breakfast clubs can give the slow start to the day that some pupils may need. Offering food and time to talk can be enough to prepare a child for a day of learning.

Medical: the special needs lead may be required to support families in engaging with medical professionals. When parents or professionals suspect conditions such as ADHD (attention deficit hyperactivity disorder) or autism are having an impact on a child's behaviour, you may be asked to write supporting letters to the GP (general practitioner) in order to initiate appropriate referrals. SENCos can also be asked to complete questionnaires that may result in a diagnosis or possible medication.

Intervention: if a child finds social situations and friendships challenging, they may need intervention to develop these skills. Small groups of peers (often including those who may model good social interaction) playing board games or being given an opportunity for structured and supported play can be the simplest means of intervention. There are also written interventions old and new, including socially speaking and time to talk, that can provide session-by-session planning. As with all interventions, the graduated approach (see page 43) should be followed.

It can be difficult to make social, emotional and mental health (SEMH) interventions measurable; however, often the most appropriate method is to use self-assessment questionnaires (pre- and post-intervention) around areas of confidence and friendship. Outcomes Star is an online system that can be used to track progress in relation to different aspects of a child's life. Tracking the impact on negative behaviour would also be an appropriate method of measuring impact as this behaviour is the reason for the intervention.

Emotional literacy: pupils who are struggling in school with behaviour often have limited emotional literacy or methods to support them at moments of dysregulation or frustration. Zones of Regulation (see page 152) is a resource that can support the teaching of emotional literacy both whole school and individually. Five-point scales and emotions charts allow children to identify how they may be feeling and why. It is supportive that adults use this to model to children how they feel.

Individual behaviour plans: many skilled practitioners in this field describe behaviours at four different stages: anxiety, defensive, risk and tension reduction. It can be useful for staff to identify triggers and signs of when a pupil's behaviour is escalating and to consider what strategies can support children at these stages. Does a job/task distract and support them? Do they need a walk around the playground with a trusted adult? If a pupil is displaying risky behaviour, a physical intervention may be needed to minimise harm to the child and others. These plans should be reviewed regularly with the team around the child and should be as personalised as possible. With all SEND plans, parents, and where appropriate the child, should be involved in co-production.

Risk assessments: if pupils are putting themselves or others at risk when dysregulated, risk assessments would be advised. Children may be physical, they may abscond, be destructive in the environment or self-harm. Risk assessments should be completed in conjunction with the parents and child, if appropriate. Risks need to be identified and support measures recorded to mitigate the risk. If pupils' behaviour is extreme, there may need to be risk assessments in place to protect the wellbeing of staff and pupils who work or are in contact with the child.

Behaviour within a school can be the difference between a calm and inclusive environment for learning or an environment which feels unsafe to work and learn in. It is not the sole responsibility of the leader of special needs to manage this; however, you will need to have a level of oversight on what you are doing to support positive behaviour within your school. This should be on both an individual and whole-school level.

ASIDE

Should a pupil with behaviour difficulties be considered SEND?

This is a question that we have been faced with continuously during our years as teachers and SENCos. It is also a question that can start a heated discussion with peers and also family members!

To an extent, it depends on your criteria. If you look at the SEND Code of Practice (2014) and are using the definition 'additional to or different from' to decide whether a child may need to be placed on the SEND register, then we would say pupils with behaviour difficulties should be on the register. Often pupils struggling with their behaviour at school need additional support to their peers in order to engage in education or remain safe in the environment. Therefore, following that definition, they would be considered to have SEND – possibly in the areas of social, emotional and mental health (SEMH) or communication and interaction.

However, staff can find this difficult to comprehend and this can be where you hear arguments such as 'They know how to behave. They are choosing not to ...', 'it's lack of parenting, there is nothing wrong with them' or 'They don't have a learning difficulty so therefore they do not need an IEP'.

If faced with these comments, we recommend you return to the Code of Practice: currently, this pupil is needing additional adult/resource/timetable support to be able to manage in school (irrelevant of the reason); therefore, they are to be placed on the SEND register.

- How will you monitor behaviour?
- How will you measure improvement in behaviour?
- How will you communicate behaviours/needs to parents?
- What can you put in place to really support a pupil who is struggling with their behaviour?
- As appropriate, what targets should be in the pupil's Education, Health and Care Plan (EHCP)?

CURRICULUM

In recent years, there has been a heightened emphasis not only on how we teach but also on what we teach – the curriculum. This shift, in our opinion, is a positive one. Delving into the content, timing and identification of core knowledge and skills for children as they progress through the education system is of paramount importance.

The curriculum is an extensive subject, encompassing not only the formal lessons but also extending to tutor time, assemblies and extracurricular activities. This chapter will focus predominantly on the planned curriculum that pupils encounter in the classroom, briefly touching on some of the peripheral elements.

As a SENCo, the expectation is not that you will be designing and planning a curriculum for pupils with SEND; this responsibility lies with the subject leader and class teachers within your school. Typically, there is a tendency to design a curriculum catering to those who can most easily access it, which is understandable. However, schools are obligated under the 2010 Equality Act and the 2014 SEND Code of Practice to ensure that pupils with SEND can avail themselves of the same opportunities as their peers. Given that the majority of time is spent in the classroom exposed to this planned curriculum, it takes centre stage. In practice, schools need to:

- establish high expectations for all pupils
- eliminate barriers to facilitate pupil achievement.

Schools are required to publish information about their curriculum and its compliance with the Equality Act and SEND regulations. This information is likely embedded in existing policies like the curriculum policy, accessibility plan, SEND policy or SEND information report. Regardless of where it resides, it should, at a minimum, cover how the curriculum is adapted, the support provided and the methods for adapting resources or providing learning aids. It is advisable to review each of these policies to ensure inclusion and alignment, as variations can occur due to different individuals drafting each policy. Using equality impact assessments can support this. Where possible, seeking pupil and parent contribution to policy is best practice.

THE ROLE OF THE SENCO IN CURRICULUM DEVELOPMENT

So, what is the role of the SENCo concerning the curriculum?

Be a source of advice and guidance:

- Expect that most, if not all, pupils in a mainstream school should experience an age-appropriate curriculum.
- Support teachers and subject leaders in identifying and delivering essential knowledge and skills, maintaining ambitious goals for individual pupils.

Incorporate the curriculum into regular monitoring:

- Schedule regular meetings with subject leaders to review the curriculum and assess its accessibility for pupils with SEND.
- When reviewing the provision, look at how readily pupils with SEND are accessing the curriculum. If a pupil is not making the progress that we would expect in a subject, we tend to look at delivery first, but at times it can be the curriculum.

There is a tendency for many teachers and leaders to put too much focus on all pupils completing the same work; children's needs are addressed just through adaptive teaching or, where appropriate, differentiated activities. This then leads to pupils, particularly those with SEN, having limited engagement with the curriculum and not being able to access it fully or learn from it.

Focusing on this aspect in more detail, how does the curriculum address gaps and/or barriers to learning effectively? In the case of pupils with SEND, these challenges may manifest as limited vocabulary, poor background knowledge, deficiencies in phonics, struggles with reading and mathematical fluency, and difficulty expressing ideas and thoughts verbally or in writing.

To support curriculum design in addressing these issues, subject leaders, with the guidance of the SENCo, could consider the following strategies:

1. **Sequencing learning differently:** rearranging the order in which concepts are taught to better suit the needs of pupils with SEN.

2. **Providing more opportunities to review and embed skills and learning:** ensuring that there are ample chances for pupils to revisit and reinforce their understanding of key skills and concepts.

3. **Personalising the curriculum:** tailoring the curriculum to accommodate the diverse learning needs and styles of pupils, allowing for a more inclusive and accessible educational experience.

4. **Adapting methods of assessment:** modifying assessment approaches to align with the abilities and challenges of pupils with SEN, ensuring fair evaluation of their progress.

5. **Focusing on subject-specific oracy skills:** emphasising verbal communication skills within the context of each subject to enhance overall understanding and expression.

Another role of the SENCo is to timetable the interventions which are available to pupils. It is vital that you ensure that the children still have access to a broad and balanced curriculum. Therefore, interventions should not always happen in the afternoon when a pupil is missing, say, geography. However, bearing this in mind, it is also important that when a pupil is accessing interventions out of class, they are not missing key learning of core subjects which may result in the gap in their learning getting bigger. Careful timetabling, which is reviewed regularly, is imperative.

OUTSIDE THE CLASSROOM

An important part of the experience for any child as they move through the school is what happens outside of the classroom. Our memories of school are unlikely to be individual lessons; they are much more likely to be the play you performed in, the sports events you attended, the trip and residentials you took part in or getting involved with lunchtime activities.

It is often the case that many of these activities are not accessible to pupils with SEND, whether in actual reality or their own perception. This can also extend to before- and after-school clubs, where staffing ratios for some pupils may close off this provision.

As a leader, first and foremost, are you aware of the number of pupils on the SEND register that attend any of these extracurricular activities? How does this compare with the numbers of pupils without SEND? For example, if you have 15% of the pupil population on the register, but only 5% of pupils with SEND attend extracurricular events, then it is worth asking yourself the question: what is the barrier for those pupils who are not attending? This analysis could also be extended further by looking at the differences between those with an EHCP and those on SEND Support, or even by looking at whether there are any differences depending on SEND need.

Numerous factors could contribute to this scenario. For instance, parents might opt to keep their child from participating if they perceive a lack of adequate support and adaptations, or do not feel confident that their child could cope in this environment. The exclusion of certain children from these activities may stem from their overall school behaviour, either as a disciplinary measure or because the activity leader restricts their involvement due to behaviour concerns. Additionally, a child's choice to abstain could be influenced by their challenges in less-structured and more-socially-oriented settings.

It is certainly worth speaking with families and, if appropriate, the child about what their barriers are and what could be done to support a higher level of engagement. You may not be able to solve every issue, but your aspiration and ambition should be that pupils with SEND are able to access a curriculum as full of experience as that of their peers, which includes the formal taught curriculum and more informal opportunities. There are clubs that are specifically designed for those with physical or cognitive disabilities, and parents should be supported to access these opportunities for their child. As a leader, it is your job to create a culture of inclusion and to challenge any decisions that may not be reflective of this.

PREPARATION FOR ADULTHOOD

An often-overlooked aspect of the curriculum for pupils with SEND in mainstream schools is their 'preparation for adulthood'.

The SEND Code of Practice (2014) states that everyone working with children and young people with SEND across education should support them to prepare for adult life and help them go on to achieve the best outcomes in employment, independent living, health and community participation. Preparing for adulthood does not rest solely with schools. Depending on the age and level of need of the pupil, social services and other areas within a local authority (LA) may be involved. For those with an EHCP, this should be discussed at annual reviews, particularly at and in the build-up to key transition points.

In practice, preparing for adulthood means preparing for:

- higher education and/or employment – this can mean looking at different employment options
- independent living
- participating in society – this includes having friends and positive relationships as well as participating in and contributing to the local community
- being as healthy as possible in adult life.

There will be many areas of the curriculum where much of this is taught or developed for all pupils, such as PSHE (personal, social, health and economic education), science lessons, tutor times and in extracurricular activities, assemblies etc. But, as has been mentioned above, pupils with SEND are often removed from some of these lessons or activities for intervention or by choice if they may not be able to access elements of the curriculum.

As a leader, it is worthwhile for you to map this provision across your school. Where are the pupils with SEND experiencing the key principles of preparing for adulthood and where are the gaps? These might be gaps for individual pupils or whole cohorts; the next step, of course, is looking at how these gaps might be filled.

In terms of future careers, all secondary pupils – and, increasingly, upper primary pupils – should be receiving high-quality careers education using the Gatsby Benchmarks. There have been some great resources produced on how to apply the Gatsby Benchmarks to pupils with SEND (https://resources.careersandenterprise.co.uk/resources/gatsby-benchmark-toolkit-send).

However, while careers education is an important element, preparation for adulthood is much broader. It should start from the early years through supporting children so that they are included in social groups and developing friendships. In primary schools, examples include staff taking pupils to the local shops to learn about money and develop their confidence, or residential opportunities that are supportive of this development.

This summary of preparation for adulthood is purposely included here in the curriculum section; if it is not planned or thought about carefully, building on what children have already done, it either does not happen or does not happen effectively. As with a number of the themes in this book, this does not mean that as SENCo you should be doing it all. Your role is to shine a light, raise the profile and importance, support, advise and evaluate the impact.

Ensuring a well-rounded educational experience for all pupils within the mainstream curriculum requires a holistic approach. As a leader in this domain, you play a crucial role in advocating for inclusive curriculum design, monitoring accessibility and promoting engagement in extracurricular activities. By collaborating with subject leaders, teachers and parents, SENCos can help bridge the gap between curriculum content and the diverse needs of learners with SEND. This includes fostering a school culture that prioritises inclusion and equips students with the knowledge and skills necessary to thrive in adulthood.

A key aspect of this is ensuring pupils with SEND benefit from the full range of curricular experiences, encompassing both formal lessons and informal opportunities like extracurricular activities and social interaction.

As mentioned above, this focus on preparing for adulthood goes beyond traditional career education, encompassing areas like independent living, community participation and healthy habits. By strategically mapping curriculum provision and identifying gaps, SENCos can play a pivotal role in ensuring all pupils, regardless of learning needs, have the opportunity to flourish within the mainstream school environment, the community and the wider world.

ASIDE

Here are some activities you could do with subject leaders to make sure the curriculum meets the needs of all students:

1. Review the curriculum together: meet regularly with subject leaders to assess the curriculum for accessibility for pupils with SEND. This involves looking at the content, delivery methods and resources used.

2. Focus on addressing gaps and barriers: identify areas where pupils with additional needs might struggle, and brainstorm strategies to overcome those challenges. This could include providing more opportunities for review, personalising the curriculum or adapting assessment methods.

3. Plan for a broad and balanced curriculum: when scheduling interventions, ensure pupils with SEND still have access to a full curriculum. Avoid taking them out of core subjects for interventions whenever possible.

4. Map the provision for preparing for adulthood: identify where and how the curriculum currently addresses preparing students for adulthood, including life skills, independent living and social participation. Look for gaps and brainstorm ways to fill them.

DISABILITY

Inclusion in mainstream schools is a vital aspect of modern education in the UK. This commitment to inclusivity extends to pupils with physical disabilities, and visual and hearing impairments. Adapting to the diverse needs of these pupils presents unique challenges. This chapter explores the types of disabilities encountered in mainstream schools, the challenges these schools might face, adaptations to the environment and curriculum, necessary staff training, and considerations regarding parental choice.

Section 19 of the Education Act (1996) is in place to support any child who cannot attend education due to illness. It puts the responsibility on the local authority to find alternative education for these children. The Department for Education (DfE) states that it is statutory for schools to have a policy regarding 'children who have health needs who can not attend school' which should be reviewed annually and approved by governors. This policy can look in greater detail at what the school will offer children who are unable to attend. It will reference the local authority offer for these children in line with Section 19.

TYPES OF DISABILITIES AND CHALLENGES

Physical disabilities: these may include conditions like cerebral palsy, muscular dystrophy or mobility impairments due to injury. Pupils at schools not specifically designed for physical disabilities might face challenges in accessibility, such as navigating staircases or narrow corridors. Schools can access short-term funding to improve accessibility for children after an accident or operation.

Visual impairments: pupils may range from partially sighted to completely blind. Challenges include accessing written materials and navigating school environments safely.

Hearing impairments: this includes a range from hard-of-hearing to profoundly deaf pupils. Challenges include communication barriers and ensuring auditory information is accessible. Position within the classroom and hearing loops can support these difficulties.

Genetic conditions: conditions such as Down Syndrome can affect a child's learning style, physical development and social skills. The challenge lies in accommodating a wide range of cognitive abilities and potential health complications.

ADAPTATIONS

Children with disability may need the support of an IEP or EHCP. An EHCP will allow for additional funding to provide adaptations, resources or training to be put in place.

Adaptations to the physical environment can include:

- ramps, elevators and widened doorways for wheelchair users
- tactile flooring and braille signage for pupils with visual impairments
- sound-amplification systems and visual-alert systems for pupils with hearing impairments
- specialised classroom furniture to accommodate physical needs.

Adaptations to teaching and the curriculum can include:

- braille or large-print books and materials for pupils with visual impairments
- use of sign-language interpreters, captioning services and hearing-loop systems for pupils with hearing impairments
- offering opportunities for children to socialise and learn from children with similar disabilities through out-of-school networks and social groups
- a modified or differentiated curriculum tailored to the learning pace and style of pupils with cognition and learning difficulties

- training for teachers in adaptive technologies and alternative communication methods.

STAFF AND SENCO TRAINING

- Regular training in disability awareness and inclusive teaching strategies.
- Specialised training in braille, sign language, Makaton and the use of assistive technologies.
- Understanding the medical and social needs of pupils with specific genetic conditions like Down Syndrome.
- Methods of monitoring the impact and effectiveness of specialist input.
- Additional adult support.
- Specialist advisory teachers can support the development of provision and offer advice to parents and staff as part of the team around the child.
- Outreach from special schools can review current provision and offer advice and best practice.
- Collaboration skills for working with healthcare professionals and therapists.

PARENTAL CHOICE

The choice for parents to enrol their children in mainstream schools is driven by the desire for inclusivity. Parents may choose mainstream settings for better social integration and exposure to diverse learning environments. Schools must communicate effectively with parents, ensuring their involvement in decision-making and adaptation processes.

Supporting pupils with physical disabilities, visual and hearing impairments, and other cognitive challenges in mainstream schools, requires a multifaceted approach but is beneficial to the school culture. It involves adapting the physical environment, curriculum and teaching methods, alongside comprehensive staff training. Recognising the unique challenges each disability presents and effectively collaborating with parents are key to creating a truly inclusive educational setting.

Such efforts not only benefit pupils with specific needs but enrich the learning community as a whole.

Parents may decide that a placement in a mainstream school is not appropriate or supportive of their child's development. If this is the case, the school will need to ensure there is an EHCP in place to enable the parents to consider alternative specialist settings. Schools or parent advice groups such as SENDIASS (Special Educational Needs and Disabilities Information Advice and Support Services) can support parents by accompanying them on visits to different schools and discussing their appropriateness.

Creating a truly inclusive learning environment for pupils with disabilities requires an approach grounded in co-production. Schools must address physical accessibility, adapt teaching methods and curriculum, and provide ongoing training for staff. By fostering collaboration between school staff, parents and healthcare professionals, mainstream schools can empower students with disabilities to thrive alongside their peers, enriching the educational experience for all.

ASIDE

Items for discussion with school staff:

- What are the biggest challenges mainstream schools face in including students with disabilities?
- How can schools ensure effective communication with parents of children with disabilities?
- Beyond physical accessibility, what are some other ways to create an inclusive learning environment?
- Describe some of the benefits of inclusive education for both students with disabilities and their peers.
- Research and share best practices for integrating assistive technologies in classrooms for students with disabilities.

EHCP

The Education, Health and Care Plan (EHCP) is the statutory document that makes provision for a young person of 0–25 years with special educational needs a legal requirement. It is necessary if the pupil's needs go beyond what a nursery, school or college can typically deliver for their pupils with special educational needs. Often schools can manage a child's provision at a SEND-support level with the graduated approach and an individual education plan allowing access to resources that are available to them.

The EHCP states the needs, provision, budget, timescales and the setting that the young person should attend. An EHCP can include health and care arrangements but only if these are in relation to education. There cannot be a plan solely for health or care need. Parents or professionals can request an EHCP from the local authority.

It is the SENCo's role to have day-to-day responsibility for the operation of SEND policy and co-ordination of specific provision made to support individual pupils with SEND, including those who have an EHCP. This does not mean, however, that you are personally responsible for the delivery of it. In most cases, this should be led by the class teacher who knows the child best.

FIRST STEPS

Before completing an EHCP, there needs to be a period of evidencing what has been trialled to support the child through the 'assess- plan-do- review' cycle. This may be resources, intervention or advice from external professionals. Evidence can be provided through IEP reviews, Team Around Me (TAM) and Early Help Assessment Tool (EHAT) meeting notes. The Code of Practice states that professionals should be involved at the early stage of SEND provision.

With advice from the local authority, assessments and subsequent reports may be requested from professionals such as speech and language therapists or occupational therapists. Their reports should offer advice on what provision for the child should include. This may involve trained staff or resources that would come at a cost to the setting. Educational psychologists can assess the level of need and make suggestions about what provision should look like. Evidence should be collected throughout a child's education, including doctor's letters, school reports, etc.

The setting needs to have evidence of the level of academic attainment and the rate of progress of the pupil. Co-production is vital to ensure that the EHCP is appropriate and identifies the pupil's needs and provision accurately.

THE ROLE OF LOCAL AUTHORITIES

While each local authority may operate slightly differently, they are bound by statutory timescales and certain processes that will be outlined here. It is the duty of the local authority to inform whether it is going to assess the need or not. If the local authority refuses to assess, then the parents can appeal through the SEND tribunal. The tribunal needs to decide whether the child 'may' have special educational needs. If it is deemed that they have, then the decision can be overturned and the local authority will be instructed to complete the assessment. Once the local authority has agreed to assess a child, it has 20 weeks from the date the request for assessment is received to produce the final plan. There can often be a delay, with this depending on the internal pressures facing the local authority.

After the assessment, the local authority must decide whether or not to grant an EHCP. If yes, it has 12 weeks to produce a draft (again there can be delays with this). If not, the decision can also be appealed through the SEND tribunal. There are several reasons why an EHCP may be refused: lack of evidence, if it is felt that the need is not enduring, or if the young person is awaiting a diagnosis.

Once the draft is received, parents have a set period of time (15 days) to review it. Parents are advised to seek the support of local SEN parental-support agencies throughout the EHCP process. At the point of reviewing the draft, parents may want the guidance of the school and other professionals involved.

FORMAT OF AN EHCP

EHCP templates look different in different authorities, however they must all have the following sections:

Section A is in relation to the child's story and their interests as well as the parent/carer view. This is often collected through 'all about me' sheets. If the child is non-verbal, views can be received through the use of images.

Section B is a summary of strengths and needs. This is in relation to the four SEN areas of need:

- social, emotional and mental health
- cognition and learning
- communication and interaction
- sensory and/or physical need.

The EHCP needs to rank these areas and distinguish which is the priority need.

Section C relates to health needs if linked to education. This section can be blank if not required.

Section D relates to social care needs if linked to education. As above, this can be left blank.

Sections E and F relate to outcome and provision. This will include what support is necessary, how often and who by. This is often broken down into the areas of need listed above. This needs to be specific and avoid words such as 'regular' or 'when required', as these vague terms make the EHCP less legally compliant.

Section G relates to health provision. As above, this can be blank if not required. It may be relevant to include details in this section about regular medical appointments that may support the development of the child in relation to their education. For example, details of 6-monthly visits to the eye infirmary to monitor eye condition or appointments relating to the process for diagnosis of autism.

Section H covers social care provision. This can be blank if not required.

Section I details arrangements for review. Some local authorities may request that the plan be reviewed within 6 weeks of its completion. This can support the communication between parents and the setting and create smaller interim targets that the school can be working towards. The EHCP must be reviewed at least annually either to stop it, make changes or keep it the same. For younger children, where change can be more rapid, the EHCP may need to be reviewed more frequently than once a year.

Section J details personal budget. This is an amount of money that can be sent directly to the family or young person if over 16. It may be used to fund some of the provision necessary to support the child and family, including respite care, transport costs or complementary therapies.

If a parent disagrees with the plan they can appeal sections B, F and I at tribunal.

Local authorities often use a system of banding to specify the amount of money a young person is allocated and whether they are eligible for a place in a specialist provision. Bands are not statutory and can vary across localities. There is further information on budgets in the funding chapter.

REVIEW

If part way through a year parents would like their child to transition to an alternate setting or receive additional provision, it may be that an early annual review is called so evidence can be submitted and a different setting/provision can be named on the EHCP.

It is important that throughout the year, the SENCo is using the EHCP to plan provision and assess progress towards outcomes with the support of the class teacher and any others involved in the child's provision. This will make the annual review process more efficient. If the EHCP is not being met, this could fall under judicial review.

The EHCP is a valuable resource at transition points. When pupils are entering new phases, there will be particular dates by which annual reviews need to be completed in order to support the transition. From Year 9, the EHCP should reference strategies to support the pupil into adulthood. A child with an EHCP will get priority over those without one during the admissions process. If a school is deemed full according to its planned admission number in a given year cohort, it can still be instructed to take an additional child if they have an EHCP and it is deemed to be the appropriate provision.

When planning annual reviews, SENCos should invite relevant professionals as well as parents. In some areas, representatives from the local authority SEND team may also attend (however, this will reflect the current pressures facing the LA). The Code of Practice states that an EHCP should be 'a forward-looking document that helps [to] raise aspirations'.

It is important that this meeting is strengths based and, if feasible, the young person should be included to make the plan as person centred as possible. There may be a moment at the beginning of the meeting where the young person shares something they are proud of and their likes and interests. One-page profiles can support this process. If the young person is able and above the age of 16, families do not need to be involved in the annual review.

THE ROLE OF THE SENCO

The role of the SENCo is to ensure that evidence is collected prior to the EHCP application, the correct professionals are involved and there is open and honest communication with the family. You need to ensure dates are met in terms of the statutory requirements. If the EHCP brings additional funding to the school, the SENCo would have the responsibility to allocate this appropriately. Resources may need to be purchased, staff directed and interventions planned.

A provision map can be used to record pre- and post-assessment data. This will enable you and the teachers to ascertain the quality and impact of intervention. Additionally, and particularly when considering a request for additional funding or an EHCP to support a pupil, the cost of provision can also be added. This will evidence whether a pupil is receiving more than the 'notional' budget that schools are expected to cover themselves or their EHCP funding provided by the LA. This information can also be valuable if a pupil's provision is ever reviewed at tribunal level.

The SENCo needs to ensure that what is in place is being recorded and analysed regularly so that at the point of annual review, all stakeholders can decide whether the EHCP outcomes are appropriate and the provision is what the pupil needs in order to succeed.

Those who lead on special needs can be creative when planning for children within their schools. If there is a pupil with an EHCP that needs a fine-motor intervention weekly, for example, the SENCo can add additional pupils with SEND to this group. If a pupil's EHCP states that they need 1:1 adult support during lunch and break time, it may be that that member of staff is used to support other students with SEND throughout the day.

The EHCP is a vital, legal document to allow pupils to be able to achieve in the most appropriate setting with the correct provision in place. In the end, managing special educational needs is all about skilful identification of need, skilful meeting of that need, and the careful communication of progress to all stakeholders.

ASIDE

The government report 'Special educational needs in England: Academic year 2023/24' (2024) states: 'Over 1.6 million pupils in England have special educational needs'.

This is an increase of 101,000 from 2023 and includes the number of pupils with an EHCP and the number of pupils with SEND Support, both of which continue a trend of increases since 2016.

- The percentage of pupils with an EHCP has increased to 4.8%, from 4.3% in 2023.
- The percentage of pupils with SEND (SEND Support) but no EHCP has increased to 13.6%, from 13.0% in 2023.

This is something that most educators will recognise. Local authorities are pressured to meet the 20-week deadline with an ever-increasing number of requests. Often local authorities who are being scrutinised are asked to improve their early help and ordinarily available provision in order to slow and reduce the number of EHCP requests being made. Their task is not an easy one and the battle for sufficient resources is constant.

Pause for thought.

- Why are there more EHCP requests?
- Has the need of children increased?
- Are all EHCP requests valid?
- Does mainstream education still meet the needs of the majority of pupils, and does it need to look afresh at inclusion?

FUNDING

For many people, a chapter on funding would be enough to make them want to put the book down and do something far more interesting! This is completely understandable, but the work of a SENCo cannot be fully understood without a good understanding of how pupils are funded more generally and an in-depth knowledge of the specifics of SEND funding. You will need to be able to speak with confidence with other leaders in your school, your school finance team and local authority officers, and will often be the ambassador for a child requiring further resources.

All state-funded schools (academies, free schools and maintained schools) receive their funding from the government. The majority of this comes through the minimum pupil funding, which is around £4000 per pupil in primary and almost £6000 per pupil in secondary schools. In addition, schools will receive additional money, depending on the cohort, for example Pupil Premium (PP) and Sports Premium.

Every local authority receives an allocation of money from the DfE/ Education Skills and Funding Agency (ESFA) for its higher-needs funding. It can then decide how much of this is set aside to place children in special schools, provide top-up funding to schools or for central high-needs services, such as educational psychologists.

Within this, the LAs are required to identify for each mainstream school in their area a notional amount to enable schools to meet the costs of additional support for the school's SEN pupils. This notional SEN budget is not separate from the school's overall budget, but it is an identified amount. As a result of this, the school is expected to:

- meet the costs of provision for pupils on SEN Support in accordance with the SEN Code of Practice (2014)

- contribute to the costs of provision for pupils with high needs (mostly those who have EHCPs) up to the high-needs-cost threshold, which is currently £6000 per annum.

Many local authorities have created banding systems, which aim to provide the range of funding available for children with a particular set of needs. When applying for any additional funding, the best route is through the annual review, specifically Section F where the special educational provision is specified. When a local authority creates an EHCP, it is recognition that the school cannot make the special educational provision. It is, therefore, up to the local authority to secure this, not the school.

Higher-needs top-up funding can pay for things such as:

- changes to the curriculum
- additional equipment, including IT and teaching materials
- support for small-group work and classroom assistance
- additional facilities such as dedicated SEN areas in schools.

THE £6000 MYTH

Ever since we have been in a leadership position in a school and as SENCos, we were under the impression that schools had to find the first £6000 of any provision for their pupils with SEND (SEND Support or those with an EHCP). This is partially correct but very misleading; it is so entrenched in our thinking that the vast majority of SENCos and headteachers still believe this to be the case.

Let's look at the law. In part 3, section 42, of the Children and Families Act (2014) it states that: 'The local authority must secure the specified special educational provision for the child or young person.'

The law requires that LAs provide sufficient funding so that schools can fund their SEND provision. As outlined above, the vast majority of this funding comes through the notional SEND budget which should cover up to £6000 per pupil per annum.

So, what should you do?

1. Speak to your finance team and find out how much comes into the school from this notional SEND budget.

2. For every pupil on SEND Support, use an average cost of £3000 per annum and remove that amount from the budget.

3. Divide the remaining amount between the number of pupils with an EHCP. That gives you the average funding you are receiving for each pupil with higher needs.

4. If needed, this should be up to £6000 per child.

5. If it is not £6000 per child, challenge the LA. The legal requirement sits with the LA to fund the £6000, not the school.

Local authorities have a legal obligation to provide the funding for special education provision, which means they have the right to expect accountability from us. It is legitimate for them to ask us to justify how we've spent the money and what impact it has had.

As a SENCo, it is your responsibility to provide detailed information on how the money is being spent on provision for pupils with SEND. You need to ensure that it is being used in the way it was intended and that it is having the desired impact. By evaluating the effectiveness of the provision and being transparent about spending, you can demonstrate to the local authority that the funding is being invested in the best possible way to support pupils. There are software options that can use provision mapping to assess the value of provisions provided to children in school.

When it comes to pupils with an EHCP, it is essential to prioritise the first element, which is ensuring that whatever is outlined in Section F of the plan is implemented. By law, the local authority must secure the provision, but the school is usually responsible for delivering it. However, as we saw earlier, it is the local authority that should provide the necessary financial support to make it happen. That is why it is crucial to make sure that you receive the funding you are entitled to. Without it, it can be challenging to provide the level of support that these pupils need to reach their full potential.

By working collaboratively with the local authority and advocating for the necessary funding, you can ensure that pupils with an EHCP receive the support they need to succeed. It may be appropriate to request a change in banding through an early annual review to provide evidence that the child needs additional funding. As a SENCo in a multi-academy trust (MAT), it can sometimes be difficult to understand or have all the information regarding funding as this can be unique for each trust. You need to be confident that you can answer questions around funding and have knowledge of what your pupils with SEND are receiving and how it is being used.

Assuming you have the necessary funding and resources, the final question is: how effective has the provision been? It is important to be able to confidently evaluate the impact of any additional resources and/or intervention being used. It is frustrating to come to an annual review without being able to state clearly whether or not a particular intervention has worked.

Of course, we want everything we do to be highly effective and for our pupils with SEND to make exceptional progress as a result. However, we need to be realistic and acknowledge the external factors that can impact a pupil's progress. The most powerful approach is to be able to say: 'This intervention is working well because of X, Y and Z, but this other one is not working as well as we'd hoped due to A, B and C. So instead, we're going to try something else.'

By constantly evaluating and adjusting our approach based on evidence and outcomes, we can ensure that we're providing the best possible support for our pupils with SEND.

SUMMARY

SENCos are responsible for coordinating special educational needs provision within a school. They are also responsible for ensuring that appropriate funding is allocated to meet the needs of pupils with SEND. They are held accountable – *with colleague leaders* – for the funding in several ways:

1. **Compliance with legal requirements:** SENCos are responsible for ensuring that their school is in compliance with legal requirements related to SEN funding, including the SEN Code of Practice (2014) and the Children and Families Act (2014).

2. **Budget management:** a SENCo may be responsible for managing the SEND budget for their school. This includes allocating training and resources appropriately, ensuring that funds are used effectively to meet the needs of pupils with SEND, and maintaining accurate records of spending.

3. **Reporting:** SENCos may be required to report regularly to senior leaders and governors on the effectiveness of the SEND provision in their school, including the use of allocated funding. They may also be required to provide reports to local authorities or other external bodies.

4. **Inspection:** SEND provision is inspected by Ofsted. SENCos are accountable for ensuring that their school meets the relevant inspection standards. Ofsted inspectors will scrutinise the effectiveness of SEND provision, including the use of funding, and the SENCo will need to be able to demonstrate that they are meeting the needs of identified children.

ASIDE

As mentioned in this chapter, we recommend that you try to do the following:

- Check the notional SEND budget allocation for your school.
- Estimate average costs for SEND Support and subtract it from the budget.
- Divide the remaining budget by the number of pupils with an EHCP to calculate the average funding per pupil.
- If the average funding is less than £6000 per pupil with an EHCP, work with the LA to secure appropriate additional funding.

GRADUATED

The graduated approach is necessary to ensure pupils within your school are getting what they need to make progress and to achieve age-related expectations. There are four stages in the cycle: assess, plan, do, review. This can be used every day by all teachers and should not be limited to supporting children with SEN; in fact it is the basis of good pedagogy.

By observing the children in our classrooms, we can make adjustments to our teaching to support further learning. The graduated approach is not a one-off event. It is a continuous process that is cyclical throughout a child's time in your setting and beyond. It sits alongside what some call the 'waves of intervention' model. The intervention model consists of three stages of support: universal, targeted and specialist.

The universal offer is what your school offers to every pupil to ensure success. This would include quality-first teaching, resources to support learning and visuals. It may also include small-group work and standard adaptation of lessons to allow pupils to access the learning. We present this model for ease of reference:

SPECIALIST

TARGETED

UNIVERSAL
QUALITY-FIRST TEACHING
ORDINARILY AVAILABLE

The graduated approach

Ordinarily available provision is devised by local authorities and highlights what should be available through the universal offer to pupils in schools within their area. It can include information on free outreach services, resources, transition systems and what should be evident in all classrooms.

Early identification of SEND is important. Schools should be listening to the views of the parent. It can be that a child presents with having difficulties at home and not in school and vice versa. SENCos, particularly in bigger schools, may have systems in place to enable parents and staff to raise their concerns. SENCos must ensure this starts with 'What have you already tried?'. If a child is not making expected progress or has difficulties that require them to have support that is additional to or different from their peers, these pupils should be on the SEND register and would need targeted intervention.

From the assess-plan-do-review model, 'do' is the process of the school working in consultation with the pupil and parents to consider what targeted support may consist of. This could be an additional daily phonics group, fine-motor intervention or a social-skills group.

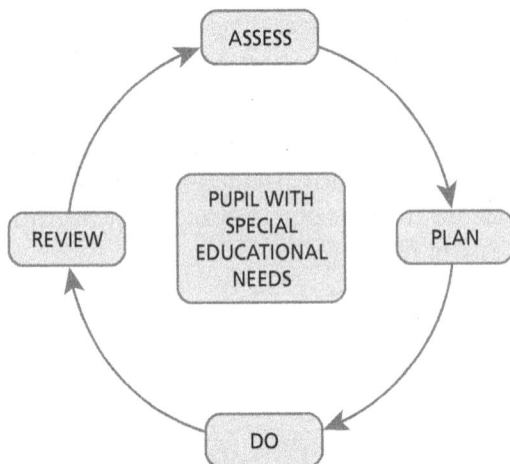

The assess-plan-do-review cycle

Targeted support may also involve professionals who are part of the school's make-up, such as an educational psychologist. The goal of targeted support is to remove barriers to learning. Timescales should be planned in terms of when interventions will be reviewed and what impact stakeholders are expecting to see. Although the SENCo needs to have an overview of the provision in place for a pupil, the class teacher must be aware of the 'plan' and facilitate the 'do' in line with the guidance.

A provision map is a vital tool. Its most basic function allows you to demonstrate what is in place across a year group or the school to support pupils with SEND. You can add information to the provision map around who, where, when to make it even more detailed and purposeful. It can also be beneficial to add details about whether the pupils accessing the intervention are School Support, EHCP or non-SEND. Adding pre- and post-intervention data to a provision map allows a SENCo to analyse impact easily.

It is important that the interventions being chosen are evidence based. You may, with fresh eyes, feel it best to put some form of intervention in place rather than do nothing. This risks staff using resources that are available rather than appropriate! It would be a good idea to speak to other leaders within your local area or trust about what resources or interventions they use to support specific barriers and what impact they are seeing. Guidance and research around the impact and value for money of interventions can be found from organisations such as the Education Endowment Fund (EEF).

It is beneficial to be part of mailing groups and to attend SENCo briefings to ensure you are up to date with current interventions that may be being trialled. Once a SENCo has been in post for a while, they will have a bank of interventions and resources that should support pupils with various needs. We present this as follows:

If a child is not making progress when accessing targeted intervention, they may require specialist support. This may be outreach from a local special school who have more specific knowledge about certain disabilities. Specialist support could also include a referral to a medical professional, such as CAMHS (the Child and Adolescent Mental Health Service), occupational therapy, or speech and language therapy. At this point, families may want to consider an EHCP.

ASSESS

Assessment is one of the four areas of the graduated approach. It allows the class teacher and SENCo to review provision that is in place. Although there can be a negative culture, where it can become apparent that teachers believe that pupils with SEND should be assessed and provided for by the SENCo, this is not the case. All children within a class are the responsibility of the class teacher and it is their role to teach and track an individual's progress. The gathering of assessment data should not delay provision. The universal offer should be analysed through the school's standard assessment procedures. Formative and summative assessment completed by the teachers should highlight those pupils who are below age-related expectations or are not making progress.

Pupil-progress meetings should allow teachers to discuss with senior leadership what they are planning to do to address any concerns. Best practice would ensure the special needs leader is present at these meetings. At this point, you should discuss whether it may be appropriate to add the child to the SEND register and consider targeted support. It would also be an opportunity to question whether the universal provision within a class is appropriate and offer professional support if it is not.

When a pupil is receiving targeted support, there needs to be further assessment to ensure the intervention is appropriate and is making a difference. Adults should consider the pupil's strengths as well as their areas of need. The views of parents and those of the pupil should be considered within this assessment. The graduated approach cycle is essential and often comprises a six-weekly process, thus fitting with the school terms. Although the standard assessment practices would demonstrate whether progress is being made, there may also need to be more specific assessments linked to small steps or SMART (specific, measurable, achievable, relevant, time-bound) targets. For example, if a pupil is receiving a phonics intervention, an assessment could consider how many phonemes they can now sight read confidently and how this has improved since the start of the intervention. If a pupil is part of a social group to boost their confidence, what is the points gain when the pupil completes a SEMH (social, emotional and mental health) questionnaire at the end of their six-week intervention?

REVIEW

Although not essential or mandatory in the SEND Code of Practice (2014), the IEP (Individual Education Plan) process supports the graduated approach cycle. A pupil's IEP should have SMART targets and be linked to support with a means of assessing the progress. There can also be guidance to parents around what activities they can do at home to support their child. The interventions described in the IEP should be added to the school's provision map. Pre- and post-assessments added to these documents allow the SENCo to review which provisions are making an impact and which are not.

This data can be used to ascertain whether particular staff members need support or have a strength that they could model to other staff. It also allows for pupils to be brought together across year groups if an intervention may benefit more than one pupil, therefore increasing the value for money of the provision.

Sometimes it can be more challenging to assess the impact of specialist support. Professionals will often have their own measures and methods of assessment. It is, therefore, important that you seek this information through regular meetings or contact with these professionals. If a pupil has an EHCP, the annual review process will bring professionals together, but this is not frequent enough. If a school is paying for specialist support, the SENCo must ensure the intervention is good value for money and that there is an impact. Professionals need to be held to account as we would do our teachers. At this point, you may request an increase in banding for the pupil's EHCP or additional funding for a short-term provision, service or intervention that may support the pupil to progress.

The pupil and their family should always be at the heart of the assess-plan-do-review cycle. Parents should be aware of the provision that their child is receiving and where the child sits within the 'wave of intervention' model.

Local authorities will often refer to the graduated approach and will have models and images to help explain this to parents and professionals. There will be further mention of this within the 'local offer'. This will help SENCos know what is available to the pupils in their schools within their local area. Schools themselves will have to publish their SEND offer through policies shared on the school website. This should make it clear to parents and others what is provided for pupils with SEND within the setting.

The graduated approach is a system that is in place to ensure that you as a SENCo are aware of what is working to support pupils and what the next steps are. Working to an assess-plan-do-review cycle will enable you to talk confidently about what colleagues are doing for the pupils with SEND in the school. Using the terms 'specialist', 'targeted' and 'universal' will allow professionals from different agencies to understand the point the pupil is at on their journey of educational and social progress.

ASIDE

For those working across a multi-academy trust, it can become apparent that the universal offer for pupils varies depending on the school a pupil attends. This is often due to the context of the school rather than a deliberate attempt to offer something different.

Ordinarily available provision, created by local authorities, strives to promote consistency of provision across schools in a locality. However, is this ever fully achievable?

A small rural school with fewer than 100 pupils will have limited staff and funds and this can have an impact on what is available to the pupils within that school. This same school may have a more personable and family feel which can mean a pupil's needs are noticed more quickly and managed appropriately.

An inner-city school may have limited green space and this could have a negative impact on a pupil with trauma or ADHD who needs regular opportunity to regulate in the natural environment. This same school, however, could have access to more external services as it is centrally located in a highly populated area.

- What can you do as a leader of SEND to ensure that your graduated approach is reflective of that of the other schools in your trust or local authority?
- What processes do you put in place to ensure your school is up to date with current practice?
- How do you compare your school with other schools with regards to 'ordinarily available provision'?

HISTORY

What's the old adage? The one lesson in history is that there *are* no lessons.

Most people in education, or at least those of us with a good few years in the business, say that things come round again and again. If you are around long enough, you will see the same ideas and the ways of doing things twice, if not more.

To an extent, this does not seem to be the case in the world of SEND. Thankfully, we are not using the same terminology as we did 20–30 years ago, and we are always striving to identify how we can be more inclusive. Yet, over the last 70 years or so, the aspiration of providing an inclusive education system for all pupils, despite improvements, is still elusive.

SEND provision began to be more recognisable as it is today after the 1981 Education Act, which defined pupils with SEND as children who have a significantly 'greater' learning difficulty than the majority of children of a similar age, or as children with an impairment or impairments. The Act stated that these difficulties or impairments prevent such children from making 'effective use' of mainstream provision within the local area. This is quite a leap as prior to this, children with SEND were often viewed as 'ineducable' and designated 'severely subnormal'. It wasn't until 1970 that education for this group of children was compulsory.

To help us understand the journey to where we are now, let's look a little bit further back. Prior to the 1944 Education Act, most schools (mainstream and special) were privately run or run through church charities. At this time, secondary education existed, but was not free, so children from poorer backgrounds were not able to access it. The 1944 Education Act initiated a number of changes, including free secondary education for all. Sadly, however, this did not apply to children with 'impairments'.

At this time, local education authorities (LEAs) were under a great deal of pressure to ensure that the new grammar and secondary modern systems would work. Consequently, it was considered necessary to separate as many children as possible who might be a barrier to this. LEAs were instructed to make separate provision for children with an 'impairment' – even though many believed that a number of these should be educated in mainstream provision, it conflicted with the desire to remove 'problem' children from the mainstream classroom.

In 1976, the Labour Government introduced a section in their Education Act, alongside the implementation of comprehensive schools, that stated the intention that all categories of children with disabilities should be provided for in the mainstream section, unless they could not receive adequate education in 'ordinary' schools, or the cost would be significant. This did not have any meaningful impact and, while the intentions were admirable, it did not change the perception that pupils with SEND were 'inadequate'; in other words, it is she/he that is different, at fault and who must change.

What has not, of course, changed over the years is pressures on finance. Special education, by definition, costs. In 1980, the DES (the precursor to the Department for Education, the DfE) highlighted that 'there is no possibility of funding the massive educational resources ... which would be required to enable very ordinary schools to provide an adequate education for children with serious education differences'.

THE WARNOCK REPORT

Perhaps the most significant, and the most comprehensive, review of SEND in England was the Warnock Report. This report formed the basis for the Education Act of 1981.

The Warnock Report, published in 1978, was a landmark document that reformed special education in the UK. Named after its chairperson Mary Warnock, the report advocated for inclusive education for children with SEN. It proposed a shift from segregating these pupils into separate schools to integrating them into mainstream schools whenever possible.

This may be why we can hear the less-inclusive adults of today stating 'we did not have these challenges when I was at school!'. The report emphasised the importance of early identification and intervention, suggesting a more individualised approach to teaching and support.

The Warnock Report aimed to create a more equitable education system that recognised the diverse needs of all children, and it laid the groundwork for subsequent legislation and policies supporting inclusive education in the UK.

Following this report, and under the 1981 Education Act, it became the duty of the LEAs to identify, assess and provide free full-time education for all children from the age of five to the end of compulsory education. After this assessment, the LEAs could issue a child with a 'statement'; this is the document, much like the current EHCPs, that outlines the child's needs and provides recommendations on how these could be met.

There were two other significant steps in the 1981 Act. The first was the importance of a range of professionals, including speech and language therapists, educational psychologists and doctors, in determining a child's SEN. The second significant step was the legal involvement of parents; however, this was far from perfect. LEAs generally only played lip service to parents' views. Pupils with SEND were often segregated within mainstream schools and the assessment process could last as long as 67 weeks!

The Warnock Report had some important ideas that are just as crucial now as they were back then. These include:

- the idea of parents as partners, involved in the whole process from early identification to placement process
- the importance of early identification
- creation of multi-disciplinary teams
- a greater emphasis on developing SEND practice during teacher training
- the idea that educational factors should not be confused with social characteristics.

SEN CODES OF PRACTICE

The inaugural Code of Practice for special educational needs made its debut in 1994, following the enactment of the Education Act (1993). This was the government's first publication offering guidance to LEAs, school governing bodies, professionals and parents regarding the interpretation and execution of the SEND legislation. The code encompassed advice on parental involvement, spanning medical, educational and psychological needs. Parents were encouraged to contribute their perspectives.

Gradually, the role of parents gained more support through the efforts of educational psychologists, who worked alongside them to pinpoint their child's requirements, as well as through charitable organisations and parent support groups. Nonetheless, the aspiration of the committee that made up the Warnock Report for constructive and informal partnerships with LEAs wasn't consistently realised, and it wasn't until the Education Act of 1993 that a Special Educational Needs Tribunal was established for parents to appeal against unsatisfactory or proposed provisions for their child. It was also through this code of practice that the requirement for all mainstream schools to have a named SENCo was introduced.

This was then followed by the 2001 SEN Code of Practice. As before, it was published as a guide for schools, local authorities and other educational institutions. The code provided comprehensive directions on how to identify, support and provide education for pupils with special educational needs and disabilities. Additionally, the 2001 Code of Practice highlighted the necessity of inclusive education and the principle that children with SEND should be educated alongside their peers whenever possible. It outlined the steps to be taken to create an inclusive environment and remove barriers to learning.

The code continued to emphasise the importance of early identification and intervention, advocating for a person-centred approach that takes into account the unique needs of each child. It underscored the significance of collaboration between parents, teachers and relevant professionals to create tailored education plans that address the specific challenges faced by children with SEN.

In 2009, it was agreed that a SENCo needed to be a qualified teacher and that within three years of taking the post, the SENCo must complete the National Award for SEN Co-ordination (NASENCo).

The most significant change came in the SEND Code of Practice: 0–25 years (2014). It is this document that we recognise in current practice.

The most notable changes in the 2014 Code of Practice

Birth to 25: the 2014 code covers individuals from birth to the age of 25, extending support beyond the previous age limit of 16. This aimed to ensure a smoother transition from education to adult life.

Education, Health and Care Plans (EHCPs): the EHCP replaced the Statement of Special Educational Needs. It is a single, legally binding plan that outlines the educational, health and social care needs of the individual, providing a holistic approach to support.

Joint planning: the 2014 code promotes joint planning and collaboration between educational settings, health professionals, social care services and parents, fostering better co-ordination of support.

Local offer: LAs are required to publish a local offer detailing the services and support available for children and young people with SEN in the local area.

Graduated approach: schools are expected to use a graduated approach when identifying and supporting children with SEND, utilising a range of interventions before involving external agencies.

Dispute resolution: the 2014 code introduced a mediation process to help resolve disagreements between parents and local authorities regarding EHCPs.

What stayed the same?

Person-centred approach: the 2015 version places a stronger emphasis on the person-centred approach, focusing on the needs, aspirations and views of the child or young person with SEN.

Inclusive education: the 2014 code strongly advocates for inclusive education, emphasising that children with SEN should be educated in mainstream settings wherever possible.

Greater parental involvement: parents are considered as partners in decision-making, and their views are taken into account when creating and reviewing EHCPs.

So … that's quite a jagged history of where our system once was and where it is today. Significant progress, led by many teachers and leaders and educational planners, has happened.

Clearly the way we think, support and fund pupils with SEND has improved over the last 70 years or so, but what is also clear is that there is still much to be improved upon. The *aspiration* for greater involvement of parents (who know their child the best), tailoring support for the individual, and trying to ensure that pupils are fully supported in mainstream education, is in many cases still that – an aspiration. For too many pupils it is not their reality.

ASIDE

SENCos can often face challenges from staff and parents around the increase in need of children with SEND. Unfortunately, it is not uncommon to hear such phrases as 'there were not children like this in school when I was at school' or 'these children should be at special school'.

A leader must challenge these statements and can benefit from having a scripted response to ensure that the staff and parents within their school understand the importance of inclusion and remain positive in the face of adversity.

Starters for a scripted response:

- Do you think the child's behaviour could be communicating an unmet need?
- Let's make a time so we can talk about this at greater length.
- What are the positives of having diversity within our school?
- Let's meet tomorrow or the day after and I can talk you through where we are within the graduated response to this child.

IEPS

Individual education plans (IEPs), although not mentioned in the SEND Code of Practice, are generally written by the class teacher/tutor under the guidance of the SENCo. IEPs are used if a pupil's needs are 'additional to or different from' those of the majority of their peers. An IEP allows the staff to monitor and support pupils with SEND as well as identifying the specific areas of need, for example: cognition and learning; communication and interaction; social and emotional; sensory or physical.

GENERAL PRINCIPLES

Good practice would suggest that IEPs are generally written and reviewed three times a year often alongside data-collection points or parents' evenings in the school year. This allows staff to pinpoint children who need additional support. The Code of Practice states that parents should be involved in deciding and evaluating school-based plans and provision for their child.

An IEP should be clear and easy to follow and be a working document that teachers, teaching assistants and supply teachers can pick up and follow without too much support or guidance. If a pupil has an IEP, they are considered SEND Support and added to the SEND register. This is then recorded as K on the school census returns.

What should be included?

- IEPs should contain information about what, when, where and with whom interventions to support targets will happen. This is to make interventions as foolproof as possible. An example could be:

Precision teaching, Mrs Chip, Wednesday 10am in the intervention room. This information is then added to a provision map which records what is happening across year groups for pupils with SEND and allows the SENCo to monitor children across the school.

- IEPs should consider and record how targets will be evaluated, for example by self-esteem and confidence questionnaire, number of times tables learned and used correctly in lessons, phonics assessment, pupil voice (qualitative), etc.

- IEPs often contain a section where the staff member can write about the child's strengths. For example, Billy is great at making friends and is very popular among his peers.

- IEPs may include a section relating to the child's need, professionals involved, medical information and, if relevant, any diagnoses.

SMART targets

The IEP should consist of around three targets. The targets should be 'SMART':

- **specific:** the target should be small and specific. It should be linked to the areas of need.
- **measurable:** this may be in the form of a percentage, for example 'a pupil will use the digraph "er" correctly in 80% of their independent writing'.
- **achievable:** the targets should be specific enough that they are achievable. If a child needs to learn several phonemes from set one, an achievable amount should be chosen.
- **relevant:** the target must be relevant to the child and their area of need.
- **time-bound:** the target must be reviewed to allow for progress to be monitored.

Targets may also involve specific resources that will support the child. An example of this may be a writing slope or a pencil to support fine-motor development.

Additionally, an IEP should give information to parents around activities that they could do at home to support, for example playing board games to increase the child's concentration span. Parents should also be given the opportunity to comment on the IEP, and it should be signed by the parent, child and class teacher.

For the IEP to be person centred, it is important that the child is involved. This may involve them completing a one-page profile where they can share information about what they are good at, what they enjoy and what support they would like. The IEP's academic targets could be displayed in child's speak (widgets) in their school books so they are aware of what they are working towards.

FORMAT

IEPs for a school/trust should be in a standard format, but this is dependent on what the school or trust wants and would find most useful. The SEND Code of Practice does not specify any format for school records. Different trusts may use a variety of plans and recording methods for pupils with SEND such as:

- adapted timetable plans
- co-regulation plans
- individual behaviour plans; this may allow for more specifics to be considered regarding triggers and support strategies.

Whatever plans are in place, it is important that they have purpose, are supportive of the pupil's development and are written with parents. Online recording systems such as BehaviourWatch allow IEPs to be created, stored and shared virtually. This is a good way to ensure records are kept and allow for an easier chronology to be collected.

TIME MANAGEMENT

Teaching staff may use their preparation and planning time to complete or review IEPs. Some schools may offer additional time if a teacher has multiple IEPs to complete. For early careers teachers, or people who have little experience of writing IEPs, the SENCo should support. It is your role to ensure they are created, and *curated*, to include relevant information and follow guidance. School staff may need training on how to write in an evaluative style.

Three times a year, as stated above, the IEP should be reviewed. It is beneficial to do one of these reviews at a point of transition (year group change) to allow class teachers to share information that is valuable and to allow for the pupil to continue to succeed in their new year group.

REVIEW

When the IEP is reviewed, the class teacher, alongside the SENCo, should be looking at the information that determines whether the pupil has met their targets. (This was decided at the point of writing the IEP.) This is why it is so important that the targets are SMART. If a target has not been achieved, it may be that it is not achievable and so may need to be broken down further. Alternatively, it may be that the intervention has not worked, in which case something different needs to be tried. Unfortunately, in busy schools, it may be that the intervention did not happen as regularly as hoped.

At points it would be acceptable for the target to remain, but this is not standard practice. If this does happen, the date that targets were given should be noted so progress can be tracked. You would want to see targets being achieved.

Data collected may be qualitative or quantitative (for example, the teacher has observed the pupil playing with peers in 90% of break times). Information could come from a questionnaire (the pupil has increased their confidence and self-esteem according to this questionnaire by 19 points). This information should also be added to provision maps in order to evaluate SEND provision in a school.

If an IEP has been successful and a child no longer needs support that is 'additional to or different from' that of their peers, they may no longer need an IEP. In such cases, they would no longer be considered SEN Support and would be removed from the SEN register.

If a pupil is failing to achieve their IEP targets on a regular basis, they may need more specialist support. This may be from outside agencies, such as drama therapy or occupational therapy. This information would be added to IEPs.

If a pupil continues to not achieve IEP targets and the school and parents feel the targets are SMART, the pupil may need to be considered for an EHCP to formalise support. Previous IEPs will support this process.

If a child already has an EHCP, then targets from the EHCP should be used to create the IEP as it will already have been agreed by specialists what is needed. This may be in a different format and can be called an Implementation plan. This plan can support the annual review process. It allows teachers to consider the larger EHCP targets while determining more achievable smaller targets.

In secondary schools, comprehensive plans are arguably harder to manage. A pupil may have up to 10 teachers, covering a wide variety of subjects, and so getting everyone to shape and use the plan can be a challenge.

Although IEPs are not referenced in the SEND Code of Practice, an IEP is a successful way to ensure that all staff are aware of what needs to be in place for a pupil. It allows for co-production with parents and ensures anyone working with the child can see what provision should be in place. This is not just as simple as creating an IEP. As a special needs advocate, it will be your role to monitor the implementation of IEPs across your school. If there are staff members who are not actively engaging with this process, it is your responsibility to support them to see their importance.

ASIDE

Staff can be reluctant to complete IEPs and this can be frustrating. Often this can be down to workload or teachers not understanding *why* an IEP can support the progress within their classroom. It can be tempting to complete IEPs on behalf of the teacher or offer tools – SMART target banks - to make the process easier.

Although at times a SENCo may need to be more directive, this can be disempowering to teachers. A supportive or coaching model will be much more impactful. This will ensure that learning is embedded so less time and support is needed by teachers later in the year.

- How will you quality assure your school's IEPs?
- In a larger school, how can the monitoring of IEPs be fairly distributed among the team?
- How often will you review the format of your IEPs, and with which stakeholders?

JOURNAL

A significant aspect of the SENCo's role is collecting evidence (medical information, meeting records, progress made) and thus you need effective methods of recording and storing information.

Team Around Me (TAM) and Early Help Assessment Tool (EHAT) need comprehensive notes to be written. They do not need to be a word-by-word account of what has been said, but should include the important decisions and actions that have been agreed. If a SENCo can do this as the meeting is taking place, they will save time but this is not an easy skill and comes with practice and experience.

Meeting notes should be agreed by those involved. Everything should be dated and this will allow for a clear chronology of involvement for the pupil. All information should be factual and should not include opinion. Information recorded can be used to gain EHCPs, can be taken to tribunal or requested in a Subject Access Request (SAR) or Freedom of Information (FOI) request.

It is imperative that all communications and recordings are professional and appropriate. Do not write or record something you would not want to be shared with the person you are writing it about.

You should also encourage others to record with the same level of diligence. This could be the pupil's class teacher, teaching assistant or any other member of staff working with that pupil. A good mantra is: assume that everything may be seen or read by someone else.

With the increasing use of AI, there are now many apps and websites that can do much of the transcribing of notes for you, and this can make things more efficient. Before you do this, however, make sure this has been approved by your school's IT team so that the appropriate security is in place and ensure that you have the agreement of all attending the meeting.

REFLECTION

It is important as a SENCo to be self-reflective. The day-to-day role of a SENCo involves interactions with a variety of people: pupils, parents, teachers, external agencies. Being reflective allows you to consider what worked and what did not and helps you to continue to develop.

After a meeting with a parent, you may wish to ask the parent whether they were happy/satisfied with the meeting. In doing this, you could also ask whether there were any arrangements that would support the parent further. This could include meeting virtually, inviting other professionals or a family friend for support, or providing translations.

After offering an intervention to a pupil, you will need to evaluate the impact of the intervention. How did it go? Did the child respond as expected? What could be done differently next time?

When offering training for staff, the SENCo should consider whether the staff have understood. Are they engaged? Do they know why the training is relevant to them? With staff, the SENCo could collect brief feedback slips after any SEN training. The monitoring of provision and practice post-training may also demonstrate the understanding of members of staff.

Being reflective can happen in the moment, when commuting to and from work or when having a debrief with the senior leadership team at the end of the day. Being reflective is hard. It often, but not exclusively, requires us to think of what may not have gone well. If we are not careful, it can become quite a negative thought process. Like most things, it takes practice but can be enormously beneficial. Try to also think about the things that went well. What can you learn from these that can be applied to other contexts?

Leaders can find it helpful to journal. This should not be a time-consuming practice that feels like an additional workload strain but an opportunity to develop your own professional development and improve your practice.

We interviewed a number of SENCos as part of our research for this book (see page 159). Their reflections focused on two particular points that are relevant here.

The more experienced SENCos talked about the importance of boundaries, in particular with parents. Many of the families have had a traumatic educational experience with their child and can have quite challenging home lives due to the needs of their child. You may be the first person who has properly listened to them.

When we asked what they loved and disliked about the job, there were, as you would expect, many similarities. The most common 'dislike' element was the large number of administrative tasks, which can prove almost overwhelming. Strong secretarial support for leaders of SEND is vital.

ASIDE

Some examples of journal-type questions could be:

- What went well today?
- If I could try the day again, what would I change?
- What was my best interaction?
- Who or what did I make a difference to today?
- What can I do differently tomorrow?

Having the time and space to be able to reflect with a variety of different people is vital for the longevity of this role. Such people can include:

- other educators
- other SENCos
- people involved in formal supervision or coaching
- family
- friends.

Each of these can bring a different perspective to the challenges and successes you are facing and will allow you the chance to debrief so you can progress in your role. An opportunity to get things off your chest will also mean you can enjoy periods of rest (weekends and holidays) more. This will mean you return on a Monday rejuvenated and ready to take on the next challenge.

KIND

There are many qualities that a SENCo should have. Below are a few of the personality traits that may be beneficial for someone practising or entering this special and privileged role. However, it is important to remember that a variety of personality types could make an effective leader in this arena.

Being kind: this could be the most important quality of all. You need to be kind and forgiving to yourself, and kind to the children and families in your care, while listening with empathy to the challenges they face. A SENCo should do their best to improve the outcomes for all. You also need to be kind to the staff within your school. They need to understand your vision and values and want to be part of the inclusive environment you are trying to create.

Being patient and accepting: things rarely work the first time they are tried, so it is important to have patience. Do not change plans quickly. Do not give up. Take your time and observe the results. Follow the assess-plan-do-review cycle (see page 44).

Being understanding: do not judge! Listen with understanding. Put yourself in the shoes of parents and teachers you are supporting. It is not easy being a parent of a child with SEND and although you may not have direct experience of this, it is important to be understanding.

Being tenacious: follow processes, keep records and, when things do not go as planned or you haven't heard back from an external agency, follow it up. Persevere!

Developing resilience: sometimes, no matter how hard you work for a child or their family, there may still be some that seem ungrateful or who do not feel you are doing enough to support them. You must be resilient. Often in this role you are asked to support and manage behaviour. It is vital that you are able to rationally detach and remain professional at all times. Every day is a new day.

Being creative: thinking creatively about staffing and resources will support the pupils and staff within your school.

Be organised: ensuring you have methods of recording and storing paperwork that is tracking what is in place for children. This will make your role easier and more effective.

Being knowledgeable: you do not need to know everything. However, you need to be willing to spend time growing your knowledge and sharing it in an appropriate manner.

Being confident: whether sharing a new initiative with staff or talking to parents, you need to be confident. Exuding confidence allows staff, pupils and families to have trust in what you are doing.

Being curious: do not give up; keep looking for solutions. Ask curious questions and trial a variety of options to support your pupils.

Be passionate: having passion about supporting pupils with SEND will make the job easier. It will also enhance your knowledge as you read around the subject or actively meet with others to discuss best practice.

Being brave: stand up for what you believe in. One of the pivotal roles of a SENCo is raising the profile for SEND in schools and advocating for individual pupils. Sometimes this is hard, especially when you have to do this with people more senior than you. This requires courage.

Being social: by attending networks, reaching out to other leaders of special needs, or just actively talking about SEND, you will learn more which will support your children within school.

ASIDE

There are a number of different methods to find out about your personality type or leadership style. Most can be searched for online or some can be purchased. It can be useful to find out what your leadership style is before taking on the role of leading SEND. This way you can be aware of why you may react in certain ways, what behaviours can impact you, and why some approaches do not work for all staff.

Look at a SENCo that you know and work with and consider the following:

- What are their strengths?
- What are the things they find most challenging?
- How do they work with different stakeholders?
- What sort of teacher are they in the classroom and how do they get the best out of children and young people?
- What do they do to continue to develop and progress in their role?
- How would you describe their personality?

LEADERSHIP

Although many organisations, such as the National Association of Special Educational Needs (NASEN), have recommended it for some time, it is still not universal to see the SENCo on the leadership team of a school. This does not mean that all SEND leaders should be on the leadership pay scale or have the responsibilities of those that are, but having them participate in senior leadership team meetings can ensure that discussions and decisions include the voice of some of the most vulnerable members of the school community.

However, many SENCos do not view themselves as leaders within the school, and they may not be seen that way by others either. The goal of this chapter, and the book as a whole, is to inspire all current and aspiring SENCos to see themselves as vital and essential leaders in their school. Remember that your role is one of the only legally required positions in a school.

This is easier said than done, of course. Some critical questions to ask yourself are: How do you see yourself as a leader in the school? Do you consider yourself to have status equal to or greater than that of other leaders? How can you make this a reality?

Other staff members will look to you to set the tone and agenda for how the school supports pupils with SEND. Have you created and communicated a compelling vision for truly inclusive practice in your school?

At the start of the year, it is good practice that you not only review all key pupils but also set out your vision and expectations. Staff members should have absolute clarity on what these expectations are, how teaching should be adapted, and who the pupils with SEND are.

Classroom teachers should be held accountable for the progress these pupils make. Every leader should consider themselves a leader of SEND, and thus all monitoring, scrutiny and planning needs to be considered with that crucial lens.

One way you can effectively encourage inclusive practice is by outlining the language staff members should be using, such as avoiding outdated terminology like 'naughty' and 'low ability'. This requires tenacity and the willingness to challenge those who use this inappropriate language. This does not have to be in a confrontational manner.

When we first started our leadership journeys, we found this aspect very difficult and often got it wrong until developing a set of 'scripts' to draw on in these types of situations. The following script could be used if a member of staff was talking about a pupil in an inappropriate setting: 'I noticed that you said … about [name of pupil]. I really need you to speak directly to his/her classroom teacher about this, rather than in the staffroom. Thank you so much.'

Can you see how this is concise, and how it outlines your expectation clearly, but in a non-confrontational manner? Trust us, it works really well.

To address SEND leadership more holistically, consider how you are impacting the quality of education for pupils with SEND. What input or advice are you giving to subject leaders when they design their curriculum to make it accessible for all pupils while still being ambitious? How well is this curriculum being delivered and, finally, how well are pupils with SEND achieving in your school, based on their starting points?

An ambitious curriculum for pupils with SEND starts with their ability to access the full curriculum. There should be a compelling reason why a pupil with SEND is not able to do this. Initially, you should work with subject leaders to ensure that this is the case and that they share your expectations. When doing this, it is important to ensure that what you are saying is aligned with the whole-school ambition. Is there a clear statement of intent for the school's ambition in how the curriculum meets the needs of pupils with SEND? If not, how can you influence this?

However, a great curriculum on paper does not always translate to great practice in the classroom. This is where SENCos can shine as leaders. You can only do so much by creating and updating EHCPs and IEPs, deploying teaching assistants and establishing intervention groups. What matters most is the daily experience of the pupils in the classroom. Are teachers ambitious for all pupils, and are they effectively adapting teaching and learning through scaffolding, modelling and the use of additional adult support?

Try to spend as much time as possible in the classroom. This does not need to be in a formal 'observing' capacity, but just to monitor pupils with SEND or assess those pupils who have been raised as a concern by the classroom teacher. After all, you are their ambassador! This will give you a good idea of which teachers require additional support and guidance.

That, of course, requires a level of knowledge either in how to support pupils with specific needs or in what effective teaching and learning looks like. You cannot be an expert in all areas, but you will be the go-to person. So, if you do not know, do you know how to find out? Are you connected with local SENCo networks? If there is not one, can you create one? What other organisations are there that can offer help and support? Do you have contacts in your local special schools? From our personal experiences, most special schools would love to showcase what they are doing to mainstream schools.

The final element of what happens in the classroom is evaluating the impact. Is what you and the teachers are doing working? Are pupils with SEND making progress? There are various ways of doing this.

The most common way is using the assessment data that teachers provide; for many schools, this is termly for most subjects. This is a useful starting point and can provide some high-level data and possibly identify where certain subjects or classes are doing particularly well or, in some cases, not so well. However, for many pupils, particularly those with an EHCP, these termly assessment checks may not identify the small steps of progress they are making. But this does not necessarily mean they are not making progress.

In these situations, it is in part knowing what specific targets these pupils may have, either on the EHCP or IEP, and having a good understanding of what progress looks like for that pupil. This can be assessed through your observations and those of the other adults in the class, and can be as simple as how much time they are able to concentrate on a piece of work from the start of term to the end, or other more ill-defined areas like social interactions.

Have the confidence to assess the pupils in a way that you see fit. Small steps for some learners are as important as big steps for other learners. You never want to hear of staff depressing expectations of what pupils with SEND can achieve; great teachers are characterised by the high expectations they have for *all* students.

As a result of academisation and the growth of multi-academy trusts, there may be additional roles being added to leadership. Some trusts have inclusion leads or directors of inclusion. This may add additional support to your role but could also add further scrutiny or work pressures.

There are numerous governance models across schools. Working with governors is an important part of the SENCo's leadership role. Ideally, in whatever governance structure you work in, there should be at least one governor who has the role of link governor for SEND or a similar role. This link governor should have two functions: first, to act as an advocate for pupils with SEND in the school, ensuring that decisions, policies and the strategic direction prioritise these pupils; secondly, to oversee how effective the provision is across the school. You will need to provide governors with the necessary information and regularly meet with the link governor.

The requirements of this will be different in each school and trust, but we hope that in whatever capacity you find yourself working with governors, you find it a supportive and challenging process. Remember: the governor wants to be a successful advocate!

Being a school leader in any area of the school is challenging and as a SENCo, this is no exception. Staff may turn to you to solve problems such as how to manage a 'difficult' child or one who is not making progress despite their efforts. You cannot be everything to everyone, but you can try to lead by example with empathy, always keeping the best interests of the pupils at the heart of everything you do.

ASIDE

Here is a short activity that you could do to see yourself more as a school leader.

Review the school's strategic plan and mission statement.

- Identify areas where the plan could be strengthened to be more inclusive of students with SEND.
- Consider how the SENCo role can better support achieving the school's goals for all students.

Then, develop a one-page proposal outlining these points.

- Briefly highlight areas of the plan where there is an opportunity to improve upon inclusion.
- Frame your suggestions in the context of the school's overall mission and goals.
- Propose ways the in which the SENCo can play a more prominent role in achieving these goals.

Present this proposal to the school leadership team.

- This activity can help the SENCo to see themselves as a leader who contributes to the school's overall success.
- It also demonstrates initiative and a commitment to inclusive practices.

MAGIC

It can sometimes feel like people expect you to have a magic wand! The high pressure of the educational environment means that other staff may expect you to have answers to questions instantly. Parents can have expectations that you can make changes to their child's provision with immediate effect. It is important that you have realistic expectations of yourself and share these expectations clearly with all stakeholders.

We share some real examples below.

A parent has made the decision that their child now needs to transition from mainstream to specialist provision.

It is vital that you make it clear to parents the processes and timescales that are in place for children with SEND. If a child already has an EHCP, the movement to specialist may be (but not necessarily) slightly smoother. However, it is not unheard of for a parent of a child without an EHCP to make a request for specialist, particularly when the child has a sudden change in behaviour or is at the early stages of their educational journey.

Do not make false promises. Ensure you have all the relevant information and advice from other professionals so that the parents are aware this is not a standalone decision. Plan meetings and future steps so that parents can see that you are taking their request seriously and following the process to get them what they want. Keep records of meetings and relevant paperwork to begin the process.

A headteacher wants you to ensure that a pupil with challenging behaviour does not disturb the school's calm environment.

Extensive record keeping can ensure that when you are challenged around provision, you are able to share exactly what you have done to support children. It is also important to share the impact of the changes you have made. When a child's behaviour changes suddenly, a school can feel at their mercy and the anxiety of staff can rise. You can be expected to know what to do to manage this behaviour and prevent it from happening again but this is often not the case. Telling the story around where the behaviour may be coming from, whether environmental or SEND, can support the understanding of staff and often leads to more empathy and patience.

Challenging staff on negative language being used to describe the pupil, such as 'naughty', 'choice', 'controlling' and 'attention seeking', can also improve the relationships.

An outside agency wants paperwork completed immediately so it can move forward with supporting a child with SEND.

Having a prioritised 'To do' list can help to ensure that the jobs that are essential are completed first (safeguarding is always the number one priority). If you have been asked to do something, be realistic with deadlines. Ask when the paperwork is needed and share when you hope to have it completed by.

Everyone is busy and people expect to wait for some things, but being honest about expectations allows you to prioritise further and prevents disappointment. Remember, you do not have to do everything. You may not always be the most appropriate person to complete some tasks. Therefore, it can be appropriate to delegate: high-quality secretarial support for SEND is a feature of best practice in schools.

A teacher wants to know what support to put in place for a child with a rare genetic disorder.

Again, this is about being realistic and honest. Sometimes it is best to share that, unfortunately, you do not know or have not heard of something. Reassure staff that you are going to be looking into it and that you have a plan to get the information you need by, for example, talking with a specialist. Give the staff member timescales and reassure them.

Often teachers just need to know that they are not doing anything wrong. The continued expectation of high-quality teaching will only benefit children. Assure the staff member that any information received will be shared with them. Organise a meeting to speak with the parents who can be the experts in supporting their child's needs.

A child wants to move class so they do not have to be with a child they find it difficult to work with.

Social difficulties can sometimes be the hardest to deal with. It is important to show empathy and understanding to the pupil. Here, again, be realistic about what can actually be done. Involve parents and staff in the conversation and ensure you have all the information. Is this difficulty new or something that has been ongoing? Has intervention been put in place to develop the social relationships for this pupil? Has there been a similar situation for either of these children previously?

At all points involve the pupil (age-appropriately) in the plan to let them know that you are listening and working on finding a solution. Regular check-ins with the pupil will ensure they do not feel forgotten or ignored and can avoid further difficulties such as emotional-based school avoidance.

In contrast to the above, it can also be a 'magical' experience being a leader of SEND.

- You can see children develop and learn before your eyes.
- You can be part of the process to get a child what they really need in order to flourish.
- You can support parents at their breaking point but then celebrate with them when things begin to change.
- You can see a teacher learn how to manage the specific needs within their classroom.
- You can evidence the progress of children through data and share this with management.
- You can build relationships with some of the most wonderful children and know that you are making a difference to their future.

In *The Voice of a SENCo* section of this book (page 159), we hear about the love and dislikes of the role. Reassuringly, everyone stated that what they most loved was making a difference to children's lives and seeing a child being able to do something that at first they were unable to do.

For some, this could seem like a very small step, for example being able to communicate with another child or adult or holding a pencil in a tripod grip.

The more experienced SENCos were able to see the impact of their work on the wider family, which was often something they were not expecting, and they found it incredibly rewarding. It is impossible to capture on the page the passion and enthusiasm in how each of them spoke about this, whether it was the Year 8 student who was close to a permanent exclusion with whom they celebrated their GCSE results three years later, or the family that are finally getting the support they now need.

Despite the challenges, all the people we interviewed enjoyed their role and couldn't see themselves doing other roles. It is, and we hope it will remain, an incredibly rewarding role in a school. It is a role like no other.

ASIDE

Reflecting on realistic expectations as a SENCo.

Goal: to identify areas where you might be facing unrealistic expectations and develop strategies to manage them.

Instructions:

1. Think about the different stakeholders you work with: school leadership, parents, teachers, external agencies and students themselves.

2. For each stakeholder group, consider situations where you might encounter unrealistic expectations. Here are some prompts to get you started:

   - When might a parent expect an immediate change in their child's provision?
   - When might a teacher expect you to have a magic solution for a student's challenging behaviour?
   - How might a headteacher's priorities for a student with SEN differ from yours?

3. Next to each situation, identify your own feelings and self-talk. For example, 'I feel overwhelmed when a parent asks for an immediate change because I know the process takes time.'

4. Develop strategies for managing unrealistic expectations. Consider the following:

   - Communication: how can you communicate processes, timelines and limitations to each stakeholder group clearly?
   - Prioritisation: how can you prioritise tasks and manage your workload to meet essential needs while managing expectations for less-urgent tasks?
   - Collaboration: are there opportunities to involve stakeholders in the process to build understanding and shared ownership?
   - Resource sharing: do you have resources or information you can share with stakeholders to empower them and address their concerns?

NURTURE

Some children may need something different from the mainstream classroom. For some pupils (often those with SEMH need), being within a class of 30 can be a challenge due to difficulties with emotional regulation and sensory overload. It is now not unusual for schools to offer their own form of nurture within the confines of the mainstream environment. This could be a therapeutic support base, opportunity for outdoor learning, using trauma-informed practices or a nurture class.

There are many reasons why a child may find education within the mainstream classroom challenging.

Children with ADHD can find the constraints of a classroom environment difficult and this can lead to distractable and impulsive behaviours. Autistic children can find the noisy, busy classroom over-stimulating, which can lead to dysregulated behaviour. Children who have had adverse childhood experiences may not be in a psychological place to be able to feel safe in the classroom and may require other needs to be met before learning is possible. It may also be that a child is currently experiencing something such as a bereavement which is having a significant impact on their resilience.

Generally, when talking about nurture there is reference to six principles:[1]

1. Children's learning is understood developmentally.
2. The classroom offers a safe base.
3. The importance of nurture for the development of wellbeing.
4. Language is a vital means of communication.

---

[1]   © Used with the permission of nurtureuk

5. All behaviour is communication.

6. The importance of transitions in children's lives.

You can find out more about these six principles online (www.nurtureuk.org).

NURTURE PROVISION

Nurture does not just mean a smaller class with more adults. It is important that within nurture provisions there is teaching of emotional literacy, regulation strategies and social skills. Zones of Regulation is a resource that may support this, along with simple emotions charts and adults regularly talking about how they are feeling, why and what they are doing to manage this. The goal should always be, where possible, to get children back into the classroom.

Any academic work should be planned by the pupil's class teacher and linked to the curriculum at their developmental level. It is important that children in nurture experience success in order to develop their self-esteem. The teacher should ensure that they are part of the pupil's education both through assessment but also relationally. There should be visits and time planned for the pupil to visit their classroom for certain periods of the day, such as story time or PE. Children should not be isolated from school events such as sports day, trips or class assemblies. Where possible, adjustments need to be made to allow these children to still feel part of their class and the school.

Sometimes children are not able to access the classroom due to anxiety. If this is the case, it may be supportive to stream the classroom into the nurture space. This will allow the child to feel part of the classroom and receive the same education as their peers but in a smaller and quieter environment in which they feel comfortable. The same can be done for assemblies. Nurture classrooms often need to be near an outside space as this allows children to have regular breaks to regulate and access to green space if possible.

In an ideal world, nurture classrooms would be led by a teacher; however, this is costly and often not viable. This is why a therapeutic support base may be a more economic option. This can be led by the SENCo but the day-to-day facilitation can be through highly trained teaching assistants who have an ability to build relationships with pupils who may need support.

Staffing within a support base should be consistent as children will build relationships with these adults and may struggle if the staffing changes. These teaching assistants may have accessed therapeutic training such as Thrive or Trauma Informed Schools UK (TISUK) or have trained to become emotional literacy support assistants (ELSA). Staff may also need to be aware of the risks that some of these children face. Therefore, training in physical intervention or STORM (Skills Training on Risk Management) assessment may also be necessary. Children can visit the support base for SEMH intervention or if they or staff have raised concerns about their wellbeing during the school day.

Nurture breakfast and lunch can provide quieter environments for pupils who become over stimulated in the hustle and bustle of the dining hall or playground. Nurture breakfast may support children who need a softer start to the morning or if there are concerns around environmental factors. This can be a small group inside having access to food but also games and resources to play with under the watchful eye of an emotionally available adult who can support social interactions.

Schools can put the nurture principles into their own practice by offering things like worry boxes or 'I wish my teacher knew' boxes. Safe places like dens or sensory rooms can be accessible within the environment. Staff should be trained to be emotionally available adults who understand how to actively listen and respond with empathy. A curriculum that concentrates on emotional literacy, as well as the core subjects, can support social development. There may also need to be changes made to the behaviour policy in place to ensure it avoids shaming and focuses on restorative work and natural consequences.

Multi-academy trusts across the country are increasingly creating nurture provisions for children across their schools. This means the provision can be funded at trust level and can be a resource that the schools can use. There is a concern that this may become a 'sin bin' of sorts if not monitored and managed effectively.

Some local authorities or private organisations provide nurture support that schools can use to refer into or pay for places. The child is likely to remain on the school's roll and be registered as educated off-site. Some settings may be Ofsted-registered while others are not. Settings may only be able to take children on a part-time basis (15 hours a week). If a school is referring into or paying for these services, it needs to consider whether time away from their home school will be beneficial or detrimental to the child.

Vitally, schools should quality assure these provisions, complete safeguarding checks and ask for regular visits and updates to review impact. It is important that schools keep in touch with their pupils and support reintegration if this is the plan.

When nurture is in place, as with any interventions there needs to be assessment. Which pupils are going to access this provision and how are you going to show that the intervention has had an impact? Often it is clear which pupils need nurture as without it they are unmanageable within the school setting. The behaviour policy does not work for such pupils, making them at risk of sanctions or even exclusion.

The simplest way to ascertain who may need nurture would be through behaviour-tracking systems that monitor the number of incidents over a period of time. Some schools use SEMH-style, whole-school tracking systems that can be completed termly and allow staff to see which pupils need support. Such systems can show any improvements made over the 12-week term. There are more thorough assessments that can be used to track a pupil's progress within SEMH and highlight areas of need. Examples of this include Outcomes Star, Thrive, Motional, Boxall Profile.

MASLOW'S HIERARCHY OF NEED

It is important that staff consider that behaviour is a communication of need. Adults should record behavioural incidents and consider what the antecedent/trigger may be for such a moment of dysregulation. Individual behaviour plans will allow the team around the pupil to identify different stages in behaviour; strategies that can be used to support at these different stages are vital.

Equally vital is that schools are tracking progress in relation to the pupil's area of need. If a child is not 'ready' to learn, they will not be showing academic progress. Thinking about Maslow's Hierarchy of Need (see also page 12), staff need to work on the bottom of the pyramid before moving on to pupils being able to make academic progress.

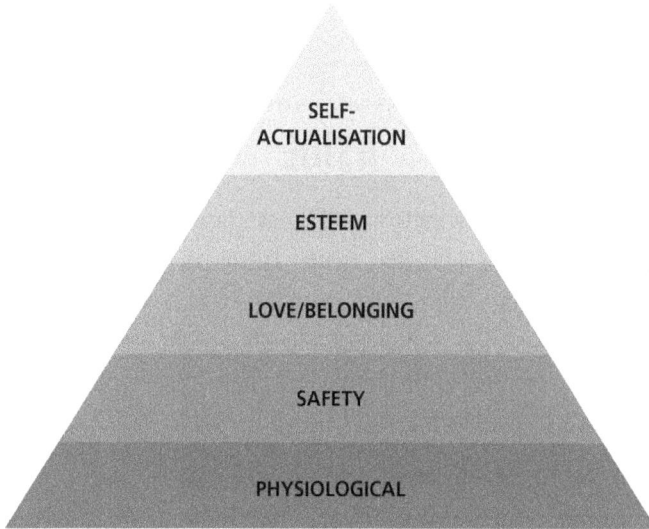

Maslow's Hierarchy of Need

If a school decides that a pupil may need something different, it is vital that this is shared with parents as stated in the Code of Practice (2014). The pupil should also have an IEP as they will be accessing something 'additional to and different from' their peers. It may be relevant for the SENCo to try to access additional funding from the local authority to fund an intervention such as nurture. Children who appear to have an enduring need where little progress is being made may need an EHCP.

If children are not progressing enough to move out of nurture provision, or are unable to manage in the mainstream classroom, it may be that they need access to specialist provision where education can be more tailored and appropriate for their needs. This should not come as a shock to parents, and conversations around this should be part of regular IEP, TAM or EHAT meetings.

The role for nurture within the mainstream setting is something that has grown over time. One of the undoubted qualities of a good SENCo is that they are naturally nurturing in the way they work with children and adults around them. They recognise and champion the fact that nurture needs to be managed and monitored appropriately to ensure it is appropriate and impactful for the children who have it as part of their provision.

ASIDE

A common challenge that leaders of SEND can face is being able to support children with behaviour difficulties. Some staff or parents can feel and share that a child's poor behaviour is being rewarded through nurture, and relational or restorative practice. This is often down to a fear of the behaviour or a lack of understanding. You need to be prepared for these challenges. Here are some conversation starters/scripts that may help.

- What is the behaviour trying to communicate to us?
- Let's complete a risk assessment for the pupil if they do/don't access nurture.
- Can we work together to think of some other strategies that may support the child?
- Since being in nurture, the pupil has had X fewer behaviour logs and has gained Y points on their SEMH assessment.
- Would you like to observe the practice in the nurture provision?

OFSTED

We understand the reality of schools and the anxiety that an Ofsted inspection can cause, especially for those leading on SEND given its high profile within the current framework. This chapter, we hope, will help you feel more prepared as well as dispelling a few myths. Please remember that no individual can impact an Ofsted judgement.

The mantra we hear from Ofsted is that school leaders should not prepare or do anything different in preparation for an inspection. To an extent this is true. We hope that by doing all the things outlined in this book, you will be ready and prepared, but we also live in the real world and you will want to make sure that you feel ready.

In Ofsted's current inspection framework, a school's SEND provision is not looked at in isolation as part of an inspection. A school is mainly looked at through its quality of education judgement and, specifically, in the design of the curriculum and how ambitious it is for all pupils including those with SEND. Ensuring pupils have access to as broad a curriculum as possible for as long as possible.

There is a comprehensive list of all the areas of SEND that inspectors would look for, many of which will be identified through the deep-dive process, specifically about being ambitious in what you want pupils with SEND to learn, whether the curriculum meets their needs and how outcomes are improving as a result of good teaching and appropriate curriculum.

Most of this inspection will be carried out through discussions with subject leaders, lesson visits, work scrutiny and meeting students. It is the work you have done with leaders and teachers prior to inspection that is going to make the difference.

You may be expected to meet with an inspector. If you feel you need to, you can have someone else with you. This could be a trust inclusion lead or a member of the senior leadership team. You are not expected to have everything in your head. In essence, what they want you to be able to articulate, in its simplest terms, is the following:

1. **How do you identify pupils with SEND?** What is the process for doing this? How do you know you are capturing everyone? How can you be sure you are not over-identifying or under-identifying pupils? What do your statistics look like against local and national data?

2. **What are you doing to support pupils with identified needs?** Be able to talk through a few case studies of a few pupils, including those with EHCP and SEND Support. What specifically is being done to support those pupils? What is the impact of this?

3. **Why are you doing this?** This element is often missed or not articulated well. No inspector will know the pupils in your school as well as you, so they will not be able to say whether that particular intervention or strategy is the right one. What they could question is whether you understand fully *why* you are doing what you are doing?

4. **What is the impact?** This is more than just national assessment results. Ofsted will not, and nor should you, compare assessment data of pupils with SEND against that of pupils without SEND, whether that be in your school or against the national average. You should, however, be looking at ways in which you are measuring the impact of the interventions you are putting in place and the progress of individual pupils, whatever that looks like for them. It will be different for each pupil. Progress could be in very small incremental steps. Remember that Ofsted are looking for you to be ambitious for your pupils with SEND and this also means in your expectation of what good progress looks like in books, folios and perhaps oral/video recordings.

Documentation that inspectors might review prior to the inspection will include the school's SEND information report, as well as the most recent inspection of the SEND services of the local authority the school is in. While you are not in control of the outcome of this inspection, it is useful to have an awareness of the main findings and how they might be impacting your school. If there are key findings, what are you able to do to mitigate against those?

QUESTIONS ABOUT SEND

What might be some of the questions an inspector asks about SEND?

1. **What is the school trying to achieve through its curriculum and how does the apply to pupils with SEND?** The most important aspect here is that what you say does not contradict with what the headteacher and other senior leaders are saying about the curriculum. Make sure you are clear on what they are saying. At the very least, all leaders need to be able to demonstrate that the ambitions are the same for all pupils, regardless of background or ability. This should be at the heart of the curriculum.

2. **How do you ensure the curriculum is designed to meet the needs of all pupils?** This could be by detailing meetings you have had with subject leaders as well as providing evidence of any monitoring you have completed.

3. **How do you make sure pupils with SEN and/or disabilities have a broad and balanced curriculum?** As above.

4. **How well do pupils with SEND access safeguarding aspects of the curriculum, such as mental health, RSE (relationships and sexuality education), consent etc.?** For some pupils with SEND this can be more challenging, so any evidence of additional work in this area is important as well as details of any training that staff may have received. For example, in any regular safeguarding training is there information provided on how to support pupils with SEND? If pupils are deliberately not removed from PSHE (personal, social, health and economic education) or similar lessons for intervention, make this point clearly.

5. **How do you support teachers in the delivery of lessons for pupils with SEN? What further plans do you have?** Detail any whole-school training you have done as well as examples of individual support provided to teachers.

6. **How do you know the curriculum is being taught effectively?** Talk through any monitoring you have done, but also any feedback you receive from other leaders who also monitor lessons.

7. **What is your monitoring of SEND telling you about the provision? What next steps were identified as part of this process?**

8. **What are the strengths and areas of development of SEND provision across the school?**

Questions 7 and 8 might have similar answers but do not be afraid to be honest here; no school gets SEN provision perfect! What you need to be confident on is that the inspectors will see the strengths and areas of development you have identified. It is also a good idea to share these beforehand with your headteacher and other senior leaders.

9. **How well are pupils with SEND progressing?** (For published data, inspectors will not ask for internal assessment data.)

10. **Looking at different groups (PP, boys, girls etc.), what do you notice?**

11. **Is there any in-school variation between subjects and why?**

12. **How well are any intervention groups/activities working?**

Questions 9–12: Data is an increasingly important element for SENCos, and while it is important to have a good grasp of this, it is also important to recognise that for many pupils with SEND, data only tells part of the picture. However, do spend some time analysing any published data. At the primary level, this could include GLD (good level of development) for reception pupils, phonics and end of KS2 data. For secondary, data could include GCSE and A-level results.

Has past data had any impact on what you are putting in place this year for pupils with SEND? What lessons have you learnt?

13. **What SEN training do staff get?** Don't just have a list of training that you have delivered, or that staff have attended. Include any evaluation and evidence of impact. This could be through any monitoring or improvements in outcomes.

14. **How does the school manage those pupils with SEN that exhibit challenging behaviour?**

15. **What steps have you taken to improve behaviour?**

Looking at these two questions together, the school's behaviour policy should be inclusive for all and outline how it manages the behaviour of all students. Reference anything additional you have put in place for children with SEMH need who are struggling to manage their behaviour. This could include nurture provision, breakfast clubs, visits out, visitors in.

16. **What are attendance figures like for pupils with SEND?** (This includes persistent and severely absent.)

17. **What pastoral support is in place for pupils with SEND?**

18. **How are specific funds for SEND allocated and spent?**

19. **What is the role of the SEND governor?**

20. **How do you ensure that pupils with SEND are safe?**

Questions 16–20 relate to whole-school matters and thus leaders at all levels will be involved in answering these. Turn to colleagues for their support; you are not alone!

This is by no means an exhaustive list. A good inspection team may well ask some, all or none of these in the exact way they have been written here. The themes remain the same, so a little bit of rehearsal may not go amiss, in line with your school's overall approach to welcoming Ofsted.

From our experience in many contexts, we would say that inspectors of SEND often learn as much from you as you learn from them – and confident inspection teams will say so!

CODA

Despite popular opinion, inspectors are not trying to catch you out. Here are a few golden rules of how to manage your inspection:

1. Do not over promise. Don't say that something is happening or is in place if it is not. This will soon be found out and it will look worse as it will demonstrate that your judgements are not sound. It is much better for you to have identified what is not working or not in place yet and tell inspectors what you are doing about it.

2. Do not be afraid to say 'I don't know' or 'I do not have that information'. Just make sure you follow up with 'but, I will find out' or 'I will get this information to you'. Follow through with this in as timely a way as possible.

3. Do not try to remember everything! There is often a fear that the one bit of information you do not have on the tip of your tongue will be the most critical. It's OK to look at notes or in a folder. An inspection is not a memory test.

4. Take someone into the meeting with you. It is good practice to take another senior leader or someone who has other information that may be useful.

5. SEND will be a thread that runs through many of the meetings with senior and subject leaders. Prior to the inspection, give your colleagues a few bullet points of what to say.

6. Use fronted adverbials: 'As a result of ... we have implemented ... and the impact has been ...'.

ASIDE

Ask a friend or a trusted colleague to go through some of these questions with you so that you can practise your responses. The more you do this, the more confident and comfortable you will be. If you are part of a trust, your inclusion lead/director of inclusion may offer SEND monitoring visits that will support your experience. Local authorities may also complete annual SEND audits which will help to prepare you for an inspection.

Additional examples of audit questions:

*   How many pupils are on your SEND register?
*   What is the biggest area of need in your school?
*   What external agencies do you use to support pupils?
*   What policies and information are on your website in relation to SEND?

PHONICS

Why include a chapter about phonics? Phonics is such a significant part of our education system, and has not been immune to controversy.

This is not, however, a chapter criticising phonics. We are both strong advocates for the approach and for the vast, vast majority of children, it is absolutely right for acquiring the English language.

However, there are some pupils who, for whatever reason, are not ready or are not able to access the current phonics programmes being used in our schools and others that sometimes get stuck. This does not mean they can never be ready or will never be able to access phonics programmes, but some pupils do not have the necessary building blocks or prior knowledge. This can stretch into secondary schools where there are pupils who are still being taught phonics, despite it having been taught to them for several years and it not having the desired impact.

Understandably, schools are reluctant to deviate from their chosen Systematic Synthetic Phonics (SSP) programme for fear of getting a negative Ofsted report or facing the wrath of their LA or MAT. Our argument is that we are failing the very small number of pupils – often those with SEN – that are not able to access phonics programmes by not giving them the building blocks they need. The ambition should always be that pupils progress onto an accredited SSP, but only when they are assessed as being ready. We need to do what is right for these pupils. In a number of cases, moving onto phonics straight away is not the right thing.

In order to understand that not all children find phonics easy, we need to understand why.

Children who find reading difficult often have one or more of these traits:

- attention and listening difficulties
- difficulties with processing, storing and articulating sounds
- challenge to recall and sequence sounds and letter names
- trouble in vocabulary learning and word finding
- difficulties in understanding and forming a range of sentences including using grammatical markers
- they are often unable to use the context to predict a word and understand what has been said
- challenge in comprehension and expression of language in words, sentences and text levels.

Reading is a skill; access to written language is required which is based on spoken language. However, it is not just spoken language written down. There is a complex code that children need to understand. This includes letters and sounds, word boundaries, grammar, intonation, stress and different styles of writing, such as fiction vs non-fiction.

SKILLS NEEDED TO BE ABLE TO READ

There are a number of skills that pupils need in order to begin to read. Some of these are detailed in the following sections.

Semantics (language)

To become fluent at reading, children need to experience language and possess knowledge and competence in understanding and using spoken language. Alongside this, experience and knowledge of the world is needed to understand and use vocabulary and emotions in context.

To support children, opportunities to model and practise communicating should be promoted throughout the whole school day in all areas of the school environment. Ideally, communication becomes a key thread throughout the whole-school curriculum as children explore vocabulary and practise using it in context.

Phonology

In order to decode words, children need an understanding of the inner structure of the words and sounds, and the rules that govern sound combinations, such as igh, ur, er, ear, air. Children with poor phonological awareness have poor language skills and find it difficult to apply language to literacy skills such as reading and writing. As a first step, children need to develop their skills in listening and attending. Pre-skill phonics/phonological awareness can help children to focus on these areas. This then helps them to to focus their attention on listening to sounds.

Understanding and use of language skills in a social context

Children with pragmatic language difficulties may also experience difficulties with fully comprehending a text as they may not grasp the context or a character's motivation or range of emotions. This lack of understanding leads to difficulties understanding the text and plot as a whole and at a deeper level.

Visual discrimination

When it comes to early phonemic development, a crucial aspect involves recognising the similarities and differences in how letters are shaped. We all know children who mix up 'b' and 'd', or have trouble telling 's' and '5' apart. This skill, often underestimated, is called visual discrimination. It starts when children are quite young, playing with toys like shape sorters, stacking cups and simple shape puzzles.

This connects with visual memory, an important skill that helps us remember visual likenesses and differences. After all, what's the use of being able to tell 'm' and 'n' apart if we forget it later? Teaching young minds to notice and remember visual content is crucial, especially in today's world where technology often does the remembering for us.

Some ideas for boosting visual discrimination and memory include:

- playing matching games and snap
- having fun with jigsaw puzzles
- gathering loose parts for creative play
- trying observational drawing and painting
- exploring 'spot the difference' or 'look and find' books.

Auditory discrimination

Phonics relies on sounds, so being able to hear the differences and similarities in spoken sounds is really important. It is not easy, especially when sounds like 'f' and 'th' sound kind of similar. This is known as auditory discrimination and involves getting ears in sync with the brain. It starts with everyday stuff; children learn it by distinguishing the sounds animals make or the sound of different musical instruments.

Matching sounds to specific items and people is an important step to achieve before diving into letters. If little ears aren't used to hearing the small stuff, like differences in sounds, it is going to be tricky matching letters with how they sound.

Children need time to mess around with making sounds using their voices, bodies, objects or even toys. As they grow and learn more words, they can copy more complicated sound patterns.

Remembering sounds

The trickiest part of learning phonics is remembering sounds, and that's really important for blending sounds later on. You might notice children who say each sound separately in a word like 'c-a-t', but then cannot remember them or blend them to say the whole word. They might say 'ca', 'at', 'ta', or even come up with their own word!

This challenge is linked to remembering sounds. For children who find it hard to remember songs, follow a complicated clapping pattern or do a two-part task, remembering a bunch of letters in the right order can feel way too hard.

Here are some ideas for improving auditory discrimination and memory:

- Sing songs together, without relying too much on visuals like YouTube. Too many pictures can make it harder for some children's brains to remember sounds.
- Read the same stories and rhymes again and again. This builds strong connections in their brains for processing and remembering what they hear.
- Organise your stories and songs from easy ones to harder ones. Start with simple rhymes like 'Twinkle Twinkle Little Star' and

work up to trickier ones like 'One Man Went to Mow'. Focus more on the order of learning, not just the topics.

- Play games like Simon Says, I Went to the Shops and I Bought ..., or quiet word games where you whisper and pass it on. These help children to hear, remember and repeat what they've just heard.

APPLYING THE TAILORED APPROACH TO PHONICS

In almost all aspects of educating pupils with SEND (and we are referring to mainstream schools here), teachers, SENCos and leaders recognise and adopt a more tailored approach to support pupils and ensure they are able to make progress. Yet in too many settings, this does not seem to apply to phonics. This could be to do with schools buying into schemes which need to be closely followed and scrutinised to guarantee the teaching of phonics, or a lack of confidence in knowing what else to offer.

In many settings, pupils struggling with phonics stay in the same groups, grappling with the same sounds and seemingly not making progress. Our conjecture for why schools do not adopt a tailored approach to phonics revolves around two possibilities:

1. an absence in training to pinpoint the reasons behind pupils lagging behind in phonics and subsequently identifying appropriate interventions
2. a lack of empowerment to implement necessary modifications.

To fix this, we need to do two things. First, give teachers the right training to understand why some pupils might be having trouble with phonics and how to help them. Second, let them have the freedom to change things around based on what they know.

We should not be afraid to challenge orthodoxies in the best interests of children with special educational needs. So often these young people demonstrate that one size does not fit all.

ASIDE

Some questions you could ask yourself about your phonics programme:

To identify students who need additional support

- How effectively are we screening students to identify those who may have underlying difficulties with phonemic awareness or auditory processing that could be impacting their progress in phonics?

- Are there students in our school who have been in phonics programmes for several years without making significant progress? If so, what data or observations do we have to enable us to understand why?

To tailor phonics instruction

- Are our phonics programmes overly rigid, or do they allow for flexibility to address the specific needs of students who struggle with traditional approaches?

- Are teachers equipped to adapt phonics instruction to meet the needs of students with SEN?

- Do we have alternative strategies in place for students who are not progressing with a standard SSP program?

QUALITY

Quality, in this respect, is referring to the quality of inclusive teaching. This is front and centre in the Code of Practice.

Paragraph 1.24 states that 'High quality teaching that is differentiated and personalised will meet the needs of the majority of children and young people ... Special educational provision is underpinned by high quality teaching and is compromised by anything less.'[2]

It continues later in paragraph 6.37: 'High quality teaching, differentiated for individual pupils, is the first step in responding to pupils who have or may have SEN. Additional intervention and support cannot compensate for a lack of good quality teaching. Schools should regularly and carefully review the quality of teaching for all pupils, including those at risk of underachievement. This includes reviewing and, where necessary, improving, teachers' understanding of strategies to identify and support vulnerable pupils and their knowledge of the SEN most frequently encountered.'

No one would argue that what happens day in and day out in the classroom is going to have the biggest impact on pupils with SEN. Just as it does for disadvantaged children or those with English as an additional language (EAL), the best teaching has a disproportionately positive impact on children with SEN. Pupils will spend around 25 hours a week in lessons with their learning directed by an adult. If this teaching is not right, then any other interventions, resources and support put in place are not going to work effectively.

---

2   *SEND Code of Practice* (2014). Contains public sector information licensed under the Open Government Licence v3.0

What, then, can a special needs leader do, through their direct work or through influencing the wider leadership team, to help create the ideal conditions to enable teachers and other adults to flourish, and provide the highest quality inclusive teaching and learning to ensure that all pupils are able to make progress?

Outlined below are some of the key, complementary elements.

ACCOUNTABILITY

Accountability links a little with culture (detailed below) in respect of what it actually looks like in practice. We are all accountable to someone or something, whether we like it or not. For some, that accountability comes from an intrinsic motivation – wanting to do what is best for the pupils and the satisfaction that brings. For others, it is an extrinsic motivation – we do things because there is an external factor making us do it. In reality, most of us require elements of both.

Paragraph 6.36 of the Code of Practice states that: 'Teachers are responsible and accountable for the progress and development of the pupils in their class, including where pupils access support from teaching assistants or specialist staff.' Most teachers know this and there is a widely used adage 'Every teacher is a teacher of SEN', but going from knowing to doing is often difficult. Accountability measures in schools tend to focus on the extrinsic motivation. SENCos are uniquely placed to support and develop teachers' intrinsic motivation, which often has a greater impact. Most of the following points focus on this.

CULTURE

Developing a classroom culture of inclusivity starts with the SENCo and their leadership and, although this cannot be done in isolation, if the SENCo is not doing it, who else will? Developing a culture can be done in several ways and will probably need a little bit of all these elements at different times and for different people.

- Allowing teachers to have some autonomy in their classrooms and enabling them, with guidance, to make decisions, empowers them to adapt their teaching methods to suit the pupils in their class and the subject they are teaching. It is important to recognise and respect their expertise.

- Sharing stories and celebrating the success when pupils with SEND have made progress and achieved, empathising the positive impact that teachers' efforts have had on pupils' lives. This will have a huge impact on the individual teachers who have done this, but also on the wider teaching team who hear these messages.

- Understanding that supporting pupils with SEND can be emotionally and, at times, physically challenging.

- Providing emotional support for teachers by acknowledging the challenges they face, offering counselling services, and supporting them in having a healthy work-life balance is really important. Often knowing they are not alone and have someone to off-load to makes all the difference.

MEANINGFUL PROFESSIONAL DEVELOPMENT

Although the situation is improving, there is very little training relating to the development of an inclusive classroom for student teachers or early career teachers (ECTs). Training is very dependent on their school placement and the quality of the mentoring they receive during their induction periods. Assuming that the base knowledge for developing an inclusive classroom is low for many new teachers, and is likely to be mixed for more experienced teachers, it is worth having a strategic and co-ordinated approach to professional development.

The starting point in making it meaningful is to offer ongoing, relevant and personalised opportunities that align with teachers' interests and needs as well as the school's priorities. There are always conflicting priorities in schools, so look for opportunities where you can provide input from a SEND perspective in any staff meetings, training sessions and whole-school briefings. If you want your trust/school to have an inclusive culture and ethos, it is good to include this and the strategies you employ to achieve this at the point of interview and induction.

How do you do each of these things? In terms of ongoing development, it is unlikely that you will be afforded frequent sessions on inclusive practice, but try to secure termly or half-termly sessions with all teachers and other adults to give consistent messages and clear expectations of how adults in the school should be supporting pupils with SEND. This will avoid ambiguity or confusion.

You can provide ongoing, regular feedback for individual teachers or departments, and this has the added benefit of being more personal. Having a more personalised approach takes longer but will have more impact. You need time to get to know some of the teachers, their expertise and areas of development as well as their interests. This can be achieved through regular monitoring.

One of the main criticisms of (poorly planned) professional development is that it is not relevant or is only relevant for a small minority of staff. By getting into classrooms, observing pupils and their learning as well as staying abreast of the latest thinking and research, you can tailor the professional development provided to meet the needs of the teachers and the cohorts of pupils. Remember, it does not necessarily have to be the SENCo delivering all the training; encouraging collaboration among teachers, allowing them to share experiences, challenges and successes, can also have a positive impact. Lesson studies and team teaching with a SEND focus can also support this.

The opportunity for class teachers to meet with the SENCo to discuss the needs within their class, and the provision they have put in place at a universal level, will ensure no pupil is missed. It also ensures that teachers know they are responsible for the pupils within their cohorts but gives the SENCo further knowledge of the pupils within their school.

INFORMATION

Schools are information- and data-rich. We are bombarded with information or requests for it and, at times, this can be overwhelming, especially for teachers. When it comes to pupils with SEND, there is often a considerable amount of information; deciding what information to share and how can be a minefield. Striking the right balance – ensuring that teachers and other adults possess sufficient information to assist those pupils in the classroom without overwhelming them and causing essential details to be lost – is challenging.

Here is a potential list of key information that teachers should be familiar with about pupils with SEND in their class:

- diagnosis and needs
- strengths and interests
- support requirements
- triggers
- behaviour support needs
- social and environmental needs
- medical needs
- EHCP/IEP
- specific targets and progress towards these
- personalised strategies
- parental insights
- outside agency involvement.

There is not much you would argue here that is not important, but if this list is provided in a pack of information at the start of the year, it is likely to stay in that pack, particularly as some teachers may have 3–4 pupils with EHCPs in their class.

One of the key skills is deciding which bits of information are critical and when. In September, it is probably more important for a teacher to know how to manage a particular pupil's behaviour so they have a positive start to the year, rather than what their EHCP target is at the end of their next key stage. That's not to say that information is not important, and you will need the teacher to know that when it comes to their annual review, but you should choose when and how that information is distributed.

ENGAGEMENT

In order for pupils to progress, they need to be engaged in the learning within the classroom and this can be more challenging for pupils with SEND. Lessons need to be interesting and varied to allow pupils to become 'hooked' and focused on the learning. Teachers can ensure engagement with a variety of tools:

- **Different questioning techniques:** ensuring that it is not only the pupils with their hands up that are involved.
- **AFL (assessment for learning):** teachers can use AFL to encourage engagement. Writing answers on mini whiteboards and showing thumbs up/thumbs down with regards to understanding. These techniques allow the teacher to adapt the teaching in the moment but can also increase engagement.
- **Resources:** manipulatives can support the learning alongside models and images.
- **Videos:** with the increase in screen time, pupils may be less responsive to videos, however having an alternate method of introducing the learning can gain a child's attention.

Although SENCos may not themselves be teaching or have responsibility for a class, they can ensure that the leadership team is monitoring the different aspects of top-quality teaching with regards to SEND during learning walks, drop-ins and observations.

ASIDE

This ten-step checklist can be used to promote high-quality, inclusive teaching:

1. Set the stage for inclusion

   - Organise a staff meeting to discuss the importance of inclusive practices and the school's commitment to them.
   - Develop a clear communication plan to share the school's vision for inclusion with parents and the wider community.

2. Empower teachers

   - Conduct a needs assessment to identify areas where teachers require additional support in implementing inclusive practices.
   - Based on the needs assessment, develop or source relevant professional development opportunities focused on strategies for diverse learners and SEND.

3. Foster collaboration

   - Create a forum for teachers to share best practice and challenges related to inclusive teaching (e.g., professional learning communities).
   - Organise peer observations with a focus on inclusive practices and provide feedback to support improvement.

4. Support teacher well-being

   - Schedule regular check-ins with teachers to discuss their workload and any challenges they face in supporting students with SEN.
   - Work with school leadership to promote strategies for managing stress and maintaining work-life balance for teachers.

5. Strengthen communication

   - Develop a clear process for sharing information about students with SEN with their teachers, focusing on relevant details and support strategies.
   - Organise regular meetings with parents of students with SEN to discuss progress, goals and any concerns.

6. Monitor and evaluate

   - Collaborate with school leadership to conduct learning walks or observations, focusing on how effectively teachers are implementing inclusive practices for students with SEN.
   - Review data on student progress and identify areas where inclusive practices can be strengthened further.

7. Celebrate success

   - Publicly acknowledge and celebrate the achievements of students with SEN and the positive impact of teachers' inclusive practices.
   - Share success stories with parents and the wider community to foster a positive and inclusive school culture.

8. Review and adapt

- Schedule regular reviews of the school's overall approach to inclusive teaching, considering feedback from teachers, parents and data on student progress.
- Based on the review, identify areas for improvement and adapt strategies to ensure continual progress in fostering a highly inclusive learning environment.

9. Stay informed

- Actively seek out new research and best practice related to inclusive teaching and SEN support.
- Share relevant information and updates with teachers to keep them informed of the latest developments in the field.

10. Advocate for resources

- Collaborate with school leadership to secure the necessary resources (e.g., assistive technology, support staff) to implement high-quality, inclusive practices effectively.

RESOURCES

In all schools, resources can be highly variable in quality and quantity, in age and beauty, in super fitness for purpose and tired irrelevance! They can help or hinder one pupil or the whole staff. They can include visuals, physical tools, software and people. When considering resources to support pupils with SEND, the special needs leader should have a grasp on the impact of these on the pupils within their school.

When choosing resources for pupils with SEND, it is important to use resources that have been trialled and tested and have measurable impact. Educational psychologists can often recommend resources which they know are beneficial for particular needs. The EEF can also measure how cost-effective some resources are.

RESOURCES LINKED TO AREAS OF NEED

Resources to support pupils with SEND can be linked to the specific areas of need.

Social, emotional and mental health

Resources that can support this area of need can be adult heavy. If a pupil is finding it difficult to manage their behaviour within school, they may need 1:1 attention or small-group work throughout the school day. If the pupil can manage without adult support, they may benefit from resources to support concentration such as wobble cushions, visual timetables and sensory resources that can be used during breaks. Interventions to develop social skills, such as R time and Socially Speaking, can provide easy-to-follow sessions for teaching assistants to run with individuals and small groups. Staff may also need training to be able to provide specific interventions such as by becoming ELSA (emotional literacy support assistants) to support pupils with their emotional literacy.

Cognition and learning

Resources to support cognition and learning may be visible in any classroom and can be a sign of quality-first teaching. Such resources can include number squares, Numicon, letter charts and word banks. However, some pupils may need more significant resources such as a laptop or 1:1 support during specific periods of the day. These resources would often be referenced on the child's EHCP.

Sensory and physical

Resources to support this area of need often come with guidance from specialists that could include occupational therapists, or visual or hearing specialists. Some pupils may need large resources such as standing desks or hoists. Schools need to ensure that their accessibility plan references these larger resources and details what the school will do to prevent the physical environment of the building becoming a barrier to pupils with SEN or disability. The accessibility plan needs to be visible on the school's website. There may also be a need for smaller resources such as worksheets with enlarged font, colour overlays, writing slants and pencil grips.

Communication and interaction

Resources supporting communication and interaction may come from speech and language therapists or specialists regarding neuro-developmental needs, such as autism. Pupils with communication difficulties could benefit from social stories, now/next charts and PECS (picture exchange communication systems). Staff often need some training before following guidance from the specialists regarding the use of specific resources.

If professionals such as speech and language therapists are coming to work with a pupil in your school, it is a good idea to allow a member of the school team to observe these sessions. This means the intervention can continue within the school day or when the specialist provision closes.

DEPLOYMENT OF STAFF

It may be that staffing and the deployment of staff are not part of your role, but if you can be part of these decisions, you can make a significant difference to the pupils within your school. These are key:

- provision mapping
- the graduated approach review of interventions
- your knowledge of pupils with SEN in your school.

All result in you having a strong idea of which staff should work with which children and which staff can provide effective interventions.

Adults are the most sought-after resource within a school and, although some pupils will be receiving funding through their EHCP, this will not cover the cost of a full-time teaching assistant. Schools need to be creative in their staffing plans.

Provision mapping can allow the SENCo to bring pupils together across year groups to provide interventions. This can ensure that the deployment of staff is effective and that it supports a high number of pupils. Some schools are creative when choosing the hours for teaching assistants and this can allow for familiar adults to be available to provide support at break and lunch time which can be beneficial for pupils with SEN, particularly those with SEMH needs.

Parents may have an opinion on what resources their child needs and why. When the fidget toy craze started, every parent felt their child needed an assortment of gadgets at their desk to help them concentrate. This was not the case for many and often led to more distraction within the classroom. However, parents should be listened to with regards to their child's SEND provision. What can be difficult is if there is disparity in what stakeholders think may support a child. If this is the case, the parents often make the final decision.

It is your role to ensure that all parties are heard and that professionals have an opportunity to share why certain decisions may be best for a child so that parents have as much information as possible to make their choices. Regular updates can also help in case there is a change of view. EHCP, Team Around the Child and EHAT meetings allow for regular information sharing for parents and professionals. It can also be beneficial to hear from the pupil, making the meeting as person centred as possible. Following the graduated approach will stop interventions or resources being used which are not making a difference to the pupil.

At the point of transition, both within school and onto alternative settings, it is vital that staff communicate what resources have supported the pupil in their class and what they will need to be able to continue to achieve into the future. It is not as simple as ensuring everything is the same year on year. With regards to resources, there may be some that children need to be weaned off as they develop to avoid over-reliance and to aid independence. This needs to be shared through the Team Around the Child meetings involving relevant professionals and parents so schools can seek the advice of others.

Impact measures will also allow the SENCo to make a decision regarding resources based on how the pupil is currently achieving and whether barriers to learning are being removed.

With regards to adult support, it can be easy to keep pupils with their 1:1 at the point of transition. This often feels like an easier option, particularly if relationships have been developed and the support is effective. However, this can make transitions onto alternative settings challenging. Staffing is also changeable and 1:1 teaching assistants could become ill, find new employment or reach retirement age. If a pupil is over-reliant on their adult, it can create turbulence in the pupil's life and development when the adult leaves. It is, therefore, sensible to have a team of staff working with pupils with SEND. This means there are at least two members of staff with whom the pupil is comfortable and who know what the pupil needs in the event of absence or change.

Your most useful resource will be a diary/calendar, whether that be paper-based, online or both. The SENCo will also be reliant on the use of an online data-tracking system to be able to identify pupils with barriers to learning and measure the impact of interventions used. There are other online systems that can create IEPs and provision maps as well as recording how cost effective interventions are. These are not essential but can support workload and encourage uniformity across a school or trust.

Since the COVID-19 pandemic, online meeting platforms have become a vital resource to support anxious families and often mean that more professionals can attend meetings as they do not need to include travel time or costs. Where possible, follow the parents' wishes with regards to the type of meeting they would prefer.

Resources come in a variety of forms. It is your role to ensure resources are sourced, used appropriately, monitored and reviewed accordingly.

ASIDE

This activity will help you assess the current state of resources for students with SEN in your school and develop an action plan for improvement.

Part 1: Resource audit

1. Categorise resources: list the various types of resources currently available in your school to support students with SEN (e.g., visual aids, assistive technology, social-emotional tools, staffing).

2. Accessibility and effectiveness: for each resource category, evaluate:

   • Accessibility: how readily available are these resources to students who need them?

   • Effectiveness: is there evidence of these resources making a positive impact on student learning and well-being?

   • Training: are staff adequately trained to use these resources effectively?

3. Gap identification: based on your evaluation, identify any gaps in resources, accessibility or staff training.

Part 2: Action plan

1. Prioritisation: prioritise the identified gaps based on urgency and potential impact on student needs.

2. Action steps: for each prioritised gap, develop specific action steps to address it.

   • This could involve acquiring new resources, improving accessibility or providing staff training.

3. Resource allocation: determine what resources (financial, personnel) are needed to implement your action plan.

4. Timeline: set a realistic timeline for each action step.

5. Monitoring and evaluation: develop a plan to monitor progress and evaluate the effectiveness of your action plan. This might involve collecting data on resource usage, student outcomes and staff feedback.

Additional considerations:

- Involve stakeholders like teachers, parents and therapists in the audit and action-planning process.
- Explore collaboration with other schools or organisations to share resources or expertise.
- Advocate for additional funding to support resource acquisition and staff training.

SENSORY

SENSORY PROCESSING DISORDER (SPD)

Although everybody has personal preferences regarding sensory input – you may struggle with loud music or find strong tastes or smells off-putting – children with Sensory Processing Disorder (SPD) have a neurological condition that affects the way the brain processes information from the senses. It can be over (hyper) or under (hypo) stimulating.

Signs that a child is hypersensitive may include them covering eyes and ears, displaying behavioural difficulties or being a picky eater. Signs that a child is hyposensitive may include them swaying, putting things in their mouth or exhibiting a high pain threshold. These signs may be strategies the child is using to try to make their senses more engaged.

Conditions such as autism and ADHD are often related to SPD. It is believed that SPD may be linked to prenatal or birth complications.

Children do not need to be diagnosed with SPD to benefit from sensory resources. Such resources could be things that are easily available for parents such as fiddle toys, ear defenders or playdough. If a child is diagnosed with SPD, they may benefit from more specialist resources often suggested by an occupational therapist. Staff can support a pupil's independence in the use of sensory resources to regulate themselves by using timers to indicate the start and end of the activity. For example, a staff member may say, 'I can see that you are feeling worried. Why don't you have 5 minutes using your regulation toy and then we will try that question again?' Now/next boards may also aid the transition between activities. Some of these resources could disturb other pupils within the class so it may be necessary to have some time out of class depending on what the resource is.

Some schools, particularly special schools, may have access to sensory areas and rooms. Sensory rooms may have bubble tubes, dim lighting, mirrors, calming sounds and soft furnishings. It is important when a mainstream school is considering developing a sensory room that it is an area that is timetabled and used to support pupils to remain regulated throughout the day. If this is not managed appropriately, it can become a room that pupils are 'put' in if dysregulated, which will encourage negative connotations and perhaps lead to further dysregulation or trauma.

ADDITIONAL SENSES

As well as the five senses (vision, hearing, smell, touch, taste), an SPD specialist may make reference to:

- proprioception, an awareness of your own body
- interoception, which relates to your internal body senses
- vestibular, which is balance.

These have a significant impact on how a child interacts with their environment.

Children should be able to have access to the school hall or a space where they can develop their gross motor skills. Exercises to support the development of the proprioceptive system in children may include holding their body weight, throwing and catching, or rolling over an exercise ball. Activities to calm the vestibular system may be similar to yoga and involve stretches and rocking motions. Interventions to support the development of interoception may include social stories or activities that can demonstrate the difference between hot and cold or can make the heart race and then calm.

The NHS website and other websites have further suggestions of supportive interventions. There are also books that have a sensory motor skills programme for staff to follow with individuals or groups of pupils. Such books include *The Little Book of Gross Motor Skills* and *Activities for Gross Motor Skills Development*. *Motor Skills United* is an occupational therapy programme providing activities and resources to help teachers develop pupils' motor skills. Details of the books are given in the References section.

Some special schools have a complex and sensory needs curriculum. These curricula allow the individual's specific needs to be met with consideration for their physical, sensory, communication and learning ability.

Sensory diet is a term that is used to plan the right amount of sensory arousal to enable a pupil to manage throughout the day. It should allow the pupil to feel calm and alert so they can then attend to the task in hand. This diet can consist of fine-motor and gross-motor activities and can help to reduce levels of anxiety. Often the strategies that the pupil uses themselves – jumping, spinning, climbing – can demonstrate the type of activity they need.

Strategies could include:

- **oral:** blowing bubbles, chewing crunchy food, sucking/blowing through a straw
- **sound:** blocking out sounds or listening to specific sounds
- **smell:** using different scents to calm or alert a child
- **vision:** removing distractions; choosing specific colours or lighting
- **environment:** using enclosed spaces or open spaces; sitting or lying down.

Sensory activities can mirror the activities that would be available in an Early Years setting: making playdough, playing with cooked spaghetti, finding things in sand.

The sensory diet for a pupil may be something that changes as they develop. There may need to be a level of 'trial and error' and therefore it is important that 1:1s or adults supporting the pupil with sensory activities keep daily notes with regards to the impact of certain activities and how they support regulation throughout the day.

If a pupil needs sensory support throughout the day, this should be recorded on their IEP with any timings along with details of the space where intervention will take place and the adult who will be leading the intervention. This will mean the provision will be reviewed at least termly but will also be available to anyone new coming to work with the child.

VISUAL-, HEARING- OR MULTI-SENSORY IMPAIRMENT

Sensory need can also refer to visual-, hearing- or multi-sensory impairment.

Visual impairment can be varied and is often linked to other medical conditions. Some visual impairment can be helped with glasses or coloured lenses/overlays and so the pupil would not need an EHCP or to be referred to as having special educational needs. Visual impairment which is more significant, however, can impact a child's development of other skills. Advice can be given by specialist teachers to support best practice within schools. This may include the use of specialist equipment.

Hearing impairment, like visual impairment, can be varied. It can be permanent or temporary but can have a significant impact on the development of other skills. Specialist teachers can help schools with their provision and advice around the equipment that is available for pupils with hearing impairment. However, some changes can be easily made such as position in the classroom, use of symbols and alternative forms of communication. It will also benefit the pupil to consider what support is in place to help them with their social and emotional development as this can be affected.

Physical need can be congenital or can result from an injury or disease. Children with a physical need may present as not making expected progress, experiencing behavioural difficulties or exhibiting low self-esteem. Some changes can be made, for example considering the layout of the classroom or the type of furniture available. This information should form part of the accessibility plan for the school. It may be beneficial to offer alternative methods of recording if the pupil has a physical condition that impacts on their fine-motor skills. Pupils should be able to access the same opportunities as their peers so specialist equipment may be necessary.

When there is a physical need that may impact the health and safety of the pupil, there may need to be additional adult support. If adult support or specialist equipment is necessary to enable the pupil to access the curriculum, an EHCP would be required.

Children with sensory and/or physical need may not need support cognitively. Therefore, it is always important that the provision is person-centred. As with all of the SEND areas of need, the voices of parents and children need to be considered.

In mainstream settings, sensory and physical need is often the least prevalent of the four areas of need. However, as a SENCo you need to have an understanding of what this can look like for children and what can be done to support them to achieve.

ASIDE

Sensory trails around a school building can support pupils who need help to maintain regulation during the day.

 Jump like a bunny 5 times

 Do wall push-ups 10 times

 Give yourself a bear hug around your chest or knees for 1 minute

An example of a simple sensory trail

Considerations:

- Is a sensory trail appropriate for all?
- Does the sensory trail need to be timetabled and/or used reactively?
- Does the sensory trail need constant adult supervision? What are the plans/ goals for pupils learning independence?
- What other professionals may be able to support with the development of a sensory trail?

TRANSITION

'A change is as good as a rest.' However, most people, if they are being honest, do not like change. The unknown can leave us feeling stressed and anxious.

For children with SEND, transitions of any size can be a challenge. There may be different reasons why a child might find transitions difficult. It could be because of an underlying neurological condition such as autism, the child may have attachment difficulties or anxiety, or there may be environmental factors that can exacerbate the challenges associated with change.

As a leader of special needs, it is important that you can predict these difficulties to ensure things can be put in place to support children at times of change.

There are many transitions within a school day. The drop-off from parents, going to lunch and moving from activity to activity are all examples. Good teachers know how important it is to manage transitions within their classroom. The transition from the carpet to the tables can be supported by silent visual cues, such as 1, 2, 3, or rehearsed routines. Schools can create regimented routines to aid transitions throughout the school day; this is recommended by the DfE (Department for Education) in the work that has been led by Tom Bennett (2020). Early morning activities are often a device used to support the transition in the morning, particularly if children have a longer period of registration. Practising routines and having high expectations can make most transitions easier. However, some children may still find them difficult.

The transition of leaving parents can be one of the most challenging. This is something that is often faced by the younger years, but if there is a specific need, it can continue throughout a child's education. If not managed carefully, it could lead to emotional-based school avoidance. Often parents are assured as their child is prised off them that the child settles within a few minutes, however this is not always the case and plans need to be made to aid the transition.

MANAGING TRANSITIONS

Transitional objects are a simple tool where the pupil may be allowed to bring something from home into school. The object could be a toy or a photograph. Borrowing items from school to bring back the next day or after the weekend can also work. Planning a sensory task that may spark interest on entry to a foundation classroom is a great way to get the pupils in and playing. Slow or soft starts with parents gradually moving away can also benefit. Pupils may find the busy transitions in the morning and at the end of the day challenging due to the hustle and bustle. In such cases, it may be beneficial to suggest that a child arrives/leaves 15 minutes late/early to avoid the rush.

For children who need more support with transitions, visual timetables showing the plan of the day or short periods of the day can lessen anxiety and allow the pupil to feel more in control. The use of a now/next board or chart can specify the transition in the moment and this can also help. Timers or wait buttons can break the change down into smaller steps so the child is prepared for when an activity will change and something new will start. Social stories can also aid transitions. These can be very simplistic with stick men drawn on a scrap of paper. The idea is that we are talking through what is happening next and why with a child to remove any unnecessary stress. This can be particularly useful if there is a change to the timetable or normality of the day.

TRANSITIONS ACROSS YEAR GROUPS AND BETWEEN SETTINGS

As there has been more experience and research with regards to transition, it is now commonplace for careful thought to be put into the transitioning of pupils across year groups. This may include planning time being given to current and future teachers to allow for knowledge and experience of pupils to be shared. For the pupils themselves, it may involve a booklet showing pictures of their new classroom and staff in the hope that any questions the child may have over the holidays can be answered. Where possible, this transition work should also include the parents who are the experts in their child.

Parents can also struggle with transition and so the more information shared, the better. It is vital that information is shared in a way that parents can access. If a child has an EHCP, they may have a 1:1 in place to support them throughout the school day and it is up to the school in collaboration with parents to decide whether this arrangement should stay the same or change as the pupil transitions through year groups. There is often argument for both cases.

Transitioning between settings is often more of a local area initiative. Systems can be used to highlight children needing enhanced, more-supported transitions. Online systems can be used to share information, however this should only be shared once a place is agreed to avoid any breaches to GDPR. Transition events, where the new school can visit the child and the child can visit their new school, can prepare pupils for the change on the horizon. Holiday activities led by the secondary school are a great way to allow children to form friendships before starting their new school in September.

For some children, transition does not need to be a grand event but opportunities throughout the summer term to allow the child to build confidence within the change can be helpful. This may include visits to the school grounds for 10 minutes with a trusted adult. Visiting the school at a time when pupils are not in can enable a child to get used to the layout. The time spent in the new school can gradually be increased.

For a child with an EHCP, it can be helpful if staff from the new school attend the annual review. The new school will then know what needs to be in place for the child as a legal requirement and the school has enough time to make plans, appoint staff and buy resources to enable this.

Schools can be inventive when planning transition-style events. In one example we were made aware of, a primary school created a day where Year 6 students were given timetables and provided with the secondary-school experience *within* the safety of their own school, visiting set teachers for set subjects. Schools that are aware that they have a large proportion of pupils transitioning from certain primary schools can plan regular events where staff from the secondary teach exciting practical science lessons or hold sporting events for the primary-aged children.

For some vulnerable children who are transitioning from mainstream to specialist education, transition needs to be planned and thorough. The transition may take weeks and could involve part-time timetables to enable the pupil to see success in their new setting.

TRANSITIONS AFTER A PROLONGED ABSENCE

If a child has experienced a prolonged period away from school, such as after the COVID-19 pandemic, 'keeping the child in mind' can be beneficial to mental health and keeping strong relationships. Tools for this may include postcards home, phone calls or video messages. This can also support a child over the summer holidays if they have difficulties with relationships.

If a child has had a period of missing education due to emotionally based school avoidance (EBSA), communication between the school, family and child is vital. Outside agencies may also need to be involved. Transition at this point may include visits from the school to the home. The importance of showing a child that home and school can work together and trust each other will support a movement back into school. A part-time timetable may be necessary to build up time in school and allow the child to experience success.

For transitions to be successful, all stakeholders will be aware of the child's needs and the strategies and provision that will support that child. This will ensure a continued positive trajectory for that child with continued progress being made. Attendance will not be an issue as all stakeholders feel confident in the move and feel it is appropriate and has been managed well.

Finally, and importantly, a special needs leader needs to be versatile and able to manage their own transitions well. Moving from, say, a conversation about the death of a beloved pet with a pupil, to a call with the local authority about EHCP funding, it is important that your time is planned and managed well so you can cope with whatever the school day throws at you. A SENCo's best friend is an online diary and a 'To do' list.

ASIDE

Transition books are a straightforward way to support pupils with and without SEN over the summer holidays. Here is a basic example.

My transition book – Year 4

In September, I will be in Year 4. My teacher will be Mr Jiwa.

I will come in this door.

I will put my coat and bag on these pegs.

A simple transition book

Points for consideration:

- Which pupils would benefit from a transition book?
- Do some pupils need additional information?
- Which stakeholders should be involved in the production of a transition book?
- At what points in the school year may transition books be needed?

UNIVERSITY

The Code of Practice states that every school must have a SENCo. They must be a qualified teacher and within three years of taking the post, they must have completed the National Award for Special Educational Needs Coordination (NASENCo) or equivalent NPQ.

NASENCo is a postgraduate course accredited by a recognised higher-education provider. The SEND qualification should be worth at least 60 credits. The NPQ in SEND is available from a variety of providers and gives the learner a mixture of online, face-to-face and research-based learning. It is the school's responsibility to ensure that the chosen qualification will allow the SENCo to achieve the outcomes and duties stated in the Code of Practice.

It can be difficult for a SENCo to complete either qualification while working full time in post. However, with careful time management and planning, you should be able to link research and academic writing to goals you have for your setting, perhaps as part of an action plan or school-development plan. If your school needs to review its behaviour policy, for example, it would make sense for you to research different behaviour strategies and use this in your assignments.

If a teacher is hoping to achieve the qualification but is not in post as a SENCo, this can bring its own challenges. Although the workload may be more manageable, it can be difficult to attain the knowledge and experience needed to complete the qualification. It may be that part of the qualification involves creating a portfolio of evidence. If this is the case, it would be advisable to work closely alongside a current school SENCo.

The qualification required to be a SENCo is something that is continuously being reviewed and may be different in certain localities. However, what is important is that as a leader of special needs, you are willing to learn and continue your professional development alongside the role.

Once in post you will be in charge of your own professional development (with the agreement of the headteacher) but also that of those you are working with in order to provide pupils with the best support while in your setting.

If a teaching assistant is working alongside a child with a medical need, for example diabetes, it would be appropriate for you to source training from external agencies such as the school nursing team or hospital diabetes team around the administration of insulin.

If a teacher is finding it difficult to manage behaviour within the classroom, it would be beneficial to source some training around behaviour strategies. However, if there is a member of staff within the trust or school who is skilled at managing behaviour, it may be more cost effective to allow the teacher to observe best practice.

If a teaching assistant is new to the school and has little experience of delivering specific interventions to support cognition and learning, it would be the SENCo's role to source training in the interventions that would support the pupils that the teaching assistant is working with. Alternatively, the TA could be allowed to shadow someone with more experience.

If, as a school, you have noticed a common area of need, for example Key Stage 1 pupils being unable to self-regulate, the SENCo may want to attend training themselves to then cascade suggestions to the team in staff meetings.

With any professional development that is taking place, it is important to consider the cost implication versus the impact. An effective way to do this is to ensure that staff provide feedback to others within the school after training. Staff can also be asked to complete an application prior to attending sessions. This will allow the senior team to ascertain whether the training is something that will have an impact on the pupils within the school. Completion of a post-training evaluation will also allow the senior leadership team to consider whether other staff members should attend the same training in the future. A good question to add to this evaluation would be: 'What are you going to put in place at X school since you have attended this training?'

In bigger schools or trusts, it would be beneficial to complete skills audits. This allows the SENCo to consider whether there are any gaps in the workforce. Additionally, the audit will support you with the deployment of staff across the school.

As with all the professional roles in education, it is vital that a SENCo has a desire to continue to learn and develop. Whether this is through additional university-level qualifications or attending a seminar on a new initiative, keeping an active awareness of your continued professional development will only improve your capacity to support those with whom you are working.

ASIDE

It is important to keep a record of the professional development you receive when you are a teacher or SENCo. Equally important is to keep a record of the professional development you direct staff to. This will allow you to audit the skills of the staff within your school and direct them accordingly. It will also ensure that staff training remains up to date, gaps are identified and filled, and details can be shared with other members of the team. The following table provides a straightforward example:

Qualification	Provider	Date	Who	Refresher?
Precision teaching	Inclusion education	23.6.23	LCS NM	NA
Safety intervention	CPI	12.5.24	LCS NM	By 12.5.25
Colourful Semantics	Communication and interaction team	14.5.24	Year 3 team	NA
Blank level	Speech and language team	17.6.24	EYFS (Early Years Foundation Stage) and Year 1	NA
Suicide prevention	STORM	21.6.24	Pastoral team	NA

VULNERABLE

It may be that you are asked to be a designated or deputy designated safeguarding lead. This can bring positives and negatives to the post.

As SENCo, it is vital that you build positive relationships with pupils and families. The challenging conversations that may need to be had as a result of safeguarding concerns are important but can damage this. However, it is also important that you know as much information as possible about the pupils within your school. This can help with provision and planning and can ensure that members of staff are proactive in response to pupils' needs.

If you are aware that a pupil is currently experiencing difficulties in the family home resulting in social work involvement, it would be appropriate to consider what opportunities there are within the school day to support the pupil with their emotional wellbeing. Could the pupil have a journal to share their worries in? Is there an emotionally available adult who can meet with the pupil daily? Is the pupil given opportunities to play and experience joy within the school day?

Pupils with SEND can be considered vulnerable not only with regards to their education but also their safety. This can be for a variety of reasons: communication, isolation, development, physical intervention. (Additional barriers can exist when recognising the abuse and neglect of any child.) These reasons are considered in turn below.

Communication: pupils with speech and language difficulties, particularly those that are non-verbal, have challenges in communicating any vulnerabilities they may be facing. The guidance document 'Keeping children safe in education' (DfE, 2024) states the importance of ensuring that children with communication barriers have appropriate support in place to avoid these difficulties.

Isolation: pupils with SEND can face vulnerability both online and offline. Children may have difficulties with social interaction and anxiety. This can result in them being isolated within their environment. Children may prefer online interaction rather than interaction in person, and this can lead to them being vulnerable if not supervised or supported in their understanding of E-safety.

Pupils with SEND may be behind their peers cognitively and can find it difficult to understand the difference between fact and fiction in online content. This can result in the pupil repeating what they have seen online in school and not understanding the inappropriateness of this.

Children can face bullying, grooming and even radicalisation online, and schools need to be confident they have the appropriate education to support this both in school and within the family home. Parents can benefit from training events, cascading of information and sharing of resources regarding E-safety.

Development: children with SEND can present at a developmentally younger age than they are. This can lead to vulnerabilities in relationships. Schools need to prioritise their relationship and sex education but also consider how this needs to be adapted for all pupils to ensure it is inclusive and developmentally appropriate.

Physical intervention: children with SEND can present with challenging and risk behaviours that could result in 'reasonable force' being used. It is vital that schools consider the risks that come from the additional vulnerability of this group of children. Schools may need to adapt their policy and practice with regards to behaviour. Involving parents and, where possible, the child in the development of behaviour plans and risk assessments is beneficial. The hope is that this should reduce the challenging behaviour, thus reducing the need for physical intervention.

As a lead in SEND, you will be working with some of the most vulnerable children in education. It is, therefore, your role to be mindful of this significant responsibility and to work in a multi-agency manner to support these children and families.

ASIDE

What are your thoughts?

Scenario one

You are observing SEND provision in another primary school within your trust or partnership of schools. You enter a classroom and your eyes are immediately drawn to a child at the back. This child is not in school uniform like the rest of her peers. She is sitting by herself and is wearing noise-cancelling headphones. While the rest of the class members are answering maths problems, this child is on a laptop researching her favourite animals. When you speak to the SENCo about pupils on the SEND register within this class, this child is not identified. When you question this, you are told 'She is a vulnerable child and social care are involved'.

- Should this child be on the SEND register?

Scenario two

A child is on the SEND register, however they are making progress and working at the expected level. The child is not showing any challenging behaviour and seems happy within school. Parents have requested an EHCP as they have challenges with behaviour at home and believe this is due to the child masking at school.

- Should this child be on the SEND register?

Scenario three

A young person has transitioned to your school after a permanent exclusion from another school.

- Should this child be put on the SEND register?

WELLBEING

PUPIL WELLBEING

As a leader of special needs, the wellbeing of your pupils should be paramount. With SEMH (social, emotional and mental health) need second only to speech and language as the most common area of need for children considered SEN ('Special educational needs in England: Academic year 2023/24', Gov.uk, 2024), the demand for support is great across the UK. Children with special educational needs often have low self-esteem and this can be exacerbated as the child gets older and the difference between them and their peers becomes more significant.

It is a good idea to assess the wellbeing of all pupils. This can be done using class audits or assessment tools such as The Boxall Profile or Motional. If schools use methods such as these, they can then offer support to the pupils presenting with the highest level of need. Children can be supported by intervention groups or resources.

If a child's wellbeing is not being supported through the universal or targeted level of support at this point, it would be essential to involve specialist agencies such as CAMHS (the Child and Adolescent Mental Health Service). Schools can either refer pupils directly to CAMHS or can write a supporting letter for parents to take to their GP for a referral. Many CAMHS services have professional and parent helplines, but they vary in response times depending on locality.

If a pupil is presenting as having low mood and is talking about suicide, then it is essential that they are seen by the appropriate services. Staff can be trained in STORM (Skills Training on Risk Management) and can then assess the risk of the child. This can be shared with health professionals and parents to see whether a safety plan needs to be created to prevent harm. A safety plan may involve ensuring medication is locked away and out of reach, keeping windows locked or removing knives, depending on the risk that is presented.

If the wellbeing of a child is low due to neglect or emotional abuse from a parent or caregiver, and is beyond the realms of early help or school support, then a referral should be made to children's social care.

It can be too easy for schools to exclude pupils with SEND from events and excursions. However, this is not inclusive and will result in poor wellbeing for those pupils and their families. Schools should prioritise assessing the risk and put things in place to ensure that all children and families are included wherever possible. This may be through providing additional staff to support a child with ADHD, or changing the location of a trip to ensure there is access for those in wheelchairs.

It could be that your school has a wellbeing or mental health lead who has been trained to support mental health within schools. The work of the PSHE coordinator also sits closely alongside this role. Creating a working party for members of staff with a vested interest in wellbeing can be beneficial for a school, especially when this group thinks about the wellbeing of all stakeholders.

Schools can also offer pupils the opportunity to become wellbeing champions. They can be voted into this role or nominate themselves. These pupils can meet with the mental health lead regularly to make plans to support the wellbeing of other pupils across the school. They could review the environment to decide whether it is conducive to learning, consider play times and what could be done to make these more positive for children (for example, the setting up of a 'buddy stop') or provide an area of quiet so pupils can avoid the noise if this helps them.

STAFF WELLBEING

When considering the wellbeing of staff, one of the most important factors is communication. This can be difficult in large organisations but can be supported by regular meetings, emails and pre-planning.

The UK government's 'Workplace health needs assessment' (2017) reviews the health of staff including wellbeing and levels of stress. Once this is completed, schools can use the information collected to offer support and information to staff on specific areas of need, such as sleep and healthy eating.

Some trusts have the opportunity to buy into employee assistance programmes. These often come with counselling and other services that can support staff wellbeing. If schools cannot afford these services, then there are free organisations such as Education Support, a UK charity that offers advice and support to school employees via a free phone line. Staff who fulfil roles that involve working with pupils who have experienced trauma or who are supporting safeguarding within their school may benefit from supervision either internally or through an external agency.

Working in schools is highly pressured and schools and trusts should write policies which demonstrate that staff wellbeing is a priority. It is becoming increasingly common to find schools employing a flexible-working policy.

Some schools, with the support of a working party, set aside wellbeing evenings for teachers where meetings will not be planned. This ensures that staff members have at least one evening a week where they can plan their own work/life priorities. Some schools also hold wellbeing days. These often form part of or the whole of an INSET day and can involve external agencies training staff on methods of wellbeing: sport, calming techniques, healthy eating. Staff members may be given an afternoon off or the chance to do something as a team.

PARENT/CARER WELLBEING

It is important that alongside the wellbeing of our staff and children we are also considering what we are doing to support the wellbeing of parents and carers. Often this is part of the role of the family support worker or parent support advisor if schools are fortunate enough to have one. Sometimes parents may need support with signposting to other agencies such as Citizens Advice or mediation services. Often parents just need a place to talk and share their worries or the opportunity to speak with other parents facing similar challenges. As a SENCo, you can facilitate a group for parents of children with SEN and invite agencies to talk to the parents about specific difficulties such as sleep or behaviour management.

Parents need to feel as though they are making a contribution to the education of their child and this can be supported by regular meetings and communications between the school and the parents. The Code of Practice states that it is valuable, if not essential, to involve parents in the reviewing of provision for their child. This can be achieved through three IEP meetings a year and report sharing. Families may also benefit from regular EHAT or TAM meetings.

Contribution may not always be specific to supporting their child; some parents thrive in helping others through volunteering or supporting the PTFA (Parent Teacher Friends Association) in raising money for the school. If the school is writing a policy which parents may have experience of, such as inclusion or transgender, it would be good practice to involve parents in the development of these policies.

If at any point you feel that the wellbeing of a parent is having a detrimental effect on their child, and the support a school can offer has been exhausted, then there should be a thoughtful and timely referral made to children's social care.

SENCO WELLBEING

Your own wellbeing as the leader of special needs should never be forgotten.

With an inbox full of emails and multiple deadlines, it is vital that you prioritise and keep an effective diary. Look ahead to see which are short-term projects and which are more long term. Make a plan of what you will do each day and have a back-up plan in case you get disturbed or directed to do something different. Try to plan one day a week where you leave your laptop in school. Remember that the holidays and weekends are there for you to rest and recuperate.

ASIDE

As a senior leader within the school, you will be acutely aware of the wellbeing of staff. Often staff wellbeing is impacted by communication or a lack of it. It is, therefore, vital that you communicate well with your team.

- Keep emails brief and succinct.
- Ensure meetings are purposeful and to the point.
- Give staff appropriate deadlines and adequate time to complete tasks.
- Provide information and advice. If you can't do it immediately, let them know when they can expect to hear back from you.
- Be available.

In looking after the wellbeing of other members of the team, you must not forget your own. Below is an activity which can support this at the end of each working day.

Before leaving work consider the following:

- What went well today? Think of at least three things.
- What challenges have you faced? How did you manage them?
- How are your colleagues?
- Are you OK? If not, what can you do about it before you leave?

Now focus on being at home – relax and refresh.

XPERIENCE

However difficult it can be at times, a leader of special needs should work collaboratively and adroitly with colleagues to gather the views of the different groups who interact with the SEND department. This includes the pupils, parents and other professionals within your community.

This information can be used as a measure of your success and inclusivity and could be collected through word of mouth or through seeking feedback via questionnaires. The information gathered can be really beneficial in supporting your professional development.

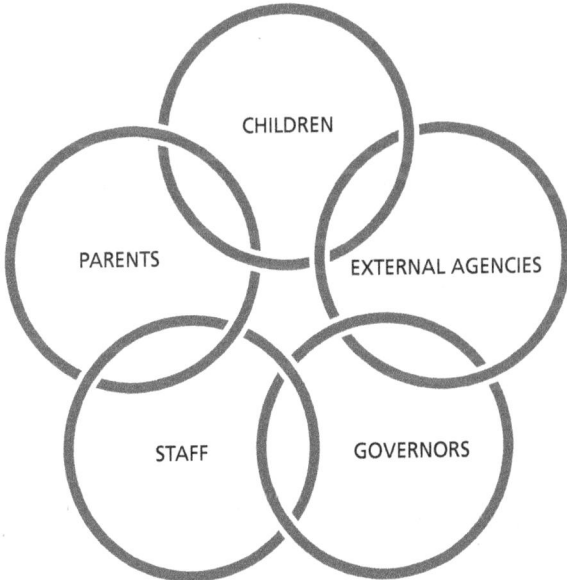

It is important that all agencies are working together to support SEND provision.

CHILDREN

The first priority should always be the children within the school. You will want all children to be making progress and feeling success within the classroom. It is the SENCo's responsibility to ensure provision is appropriate and that the graduated approach is followed. Seeking pupil voice will enable you to know how children are feeling within the setting. Appreciative enquiry is a valid method of ascertaining how a pupils is finding their school experience. If a child is non-verbal, images can be used to support this process.

Another method of judging the experience of pupils with SEND within your school is by analysing data through the graduated approach. This will show whether there is measurable impact and whether the pupils are making progress.

The experience of all pupils within the school, not just those with SEND, should be considered. How a school manages its equality, diversity and inclusion is vital and is something that a SENCo needs to be able to talk about with confidence. If a school is managing this appropriately, it will support the development of pupils into accepting and inclusive adults.

If pupils have significant SEMH needs which are having a negative impact on their behaviour, this can have a detrimental effect on the school experience of staff and pupils within the school. Having a school council or regularly seeking pupil voice will allow the school to find out whether this is a problem and how the pupils think things can be improved. Having a behaviour policy with rules and sanctions that are predictable and fair will also improve the experience of the pupils and staff in your school.

PARENTS

Although pupils are the priority, parents have to be on-board with the school's plans and give consent. It is important that parents have a positive experience of their child's time at school. Some parents struggle to engage with their child's school due to negative experiences they may have had at school. If, as a school, you work hard to make parents feel welcome (building positive relationships, hosting events which are useful and enticing), this will be passed on by word of mouth, ensuring the school continues to grow. Parents can also have their opinions heard through questionnaires, parent groups and feedback opportunities at events such as parents' evenings or class assemblies.

It is important that parents feel heard and respected as the decision-makers for their children. When holding meetings for pupils with SEND, it is helpful to ascertain from the start what the parent would like to be called throughout the meeting. Many a SENCo will refer to the parent as 'Mum' or 'Dad' and this is not always appreciated and can come across as condescending.

If the meeting has several people attending, name tags can help the flow of conversation and ensure everyone feels respected. If using acronyms, it is best to explain what each one means and check for understanding from all attendees; some school ban acronyms when talking to parents! If a parent feels anxious, it can be supportive to ask them whether they would like to invite a friend or family member. A parent's experience will also be more positive if they feel the SENCo knows their child and is working hard to support them.

EXTERNAL AGENCIES

As a leader of SEND, your job would be near impossible without the help of external agencies. It is, therefore, important that you improve their experience by giving these professionals enough notice for meetings and ensuring you are efficient with their time. Sharing comprehensive paperwork in a timely manner and, if possible, offering them a cup of tea when they attend your school will help to develop positive working relationships. We are all busy!

You will need to facilitate the annual review process. This can be a daunting experience if you have not done this before and will often involve a variety of stakeholders.

To make the meeting as successful as possible consider the following:

- Are you prepared?
- Is there information you can send out in advance?
- Have you invited the relevant people?

- Are you aware whether or not a pupil is achieving their targets? What are your plans regarding this?
- Could/should you speak to any key players (parents) prior to the meeting?
- Do you have enough time?
- Are you confident enough to take notes at the same time or do you need support with this?
- Have you included the child?
- Have you got a room that is private but comfortable?
- Are some members of the meeting joining virtually?

During the meeting:

- Make introductions.
- Ensure everybody is comfortable and that you have considered individuals' needs.
- Report on the child's progress.
- Discuss the current provision.
- Consider changes to the outcomes.
- Give everybody the opportunity to contribute.
- Summarise.

STAFF

Staff need to feel heard and supported if they are to have a positive experience working within your school. Although it adds to the workload of the SENCo, staff can be more responsive to a leader who teaches at least a part timetable. You may feel that by continuing to teach, you have credibility and can understand the pressures of teaching a whole class while also supporting those pupils with SEND. It also allows you to develop practices and trial resources before recommending them to all school staff.

Staff will have a positive experience if they feel they have autonomy for the pupils in their class and that they are involved in making decisions regarding provision for them. While some staff may be happy to take a 'back seat' when it comes to pupils with SEND, this is not what the Code of Practice advises. The responsibility for pupils with SEND is that of the class teacher. Staff will have a positive experience if they can learn more about the role of the SENCo by attending meetings regarding the pupil or supporting the SENCo to complete paperwork. This will also form part of their own professional development.

If offering training to school or trust staff on a new initiative, it can be beneficial to seek feedback after the session via anonymous questionnaire. The data can form part of your performance-management evidence if positive or provide you with an area of development if negative.

GOVERNORS

In your important role, you will need to feed back to governors on the progress and attainment of pupils. It is important to identify the gap between those with and without SEND. Is the gap growing or closing and what are you doing to have a positive impact on this? The Code of Practice references the importance of governors and highlights their role in ensuring that the Equality Act is being met.

It is good practice to have a governor who is responsible for SEND. They should visit the school regularly and observe the provision that is in place. They can then provide feedback to other members of the governing board. It would be beneficial for them to be informed of the staff, parent and pupil feedback and to look for evidence of this during their visits into school. To improve the experience of the governors, offer them information that is easy to understand and concise as they are not always experts in education.

While considering all of the above, you also need to think about the experience you are having professionally and personally. Do you enjoy the role? Do you have enough time? Are you having an impact? What are your next steps? Is there any further training or development that would help you to improve?

These questions should be discussed during performance management. An open and honest relationship with the senior leadership team can result in systemic changes that may make your job more impactful, thereby supporting your own wellbeing and enjoyment of the role.

ASIDE

What experience is essential for you to be a successful SENCo?	True	False
NASENCo or NPQSEN		
Experience of teaching every year group/age within your setting		
Your own children with SEN		
Experience of working with children or adults with SEN out of the education environment		
Previous subject leadership		
5 years or more teaching		
Experience of teaching in a specialist setting		

There is *not* an essential list of experience you need to be a successful leader of special educational needs and disabilities. There are some things that may make it an easier role for you to step into; so much of it can and will be learned on the job.

YEARNING

Our schooling system is currently wrestling with a significant rise in pupils in mainstream schools with identified special educational needs. We need teachers and support staff to step up to the challenges this presents. Indeed, we need staff *yearning* to lead SEND in a wide range of settings, from early years through to further education.

The role of the SENCo is varied depending on the setting you are in. Some SENCos carry out the role in addition to their day-to-day teaching (or the other way round, depending on how you think about it) with maybe only half a day non-contact time. Others may work full time as a SENCo and have no teaching responsibility. This decision would be made by the trust or school and is often based on need; in other words, the number of pupils with EHCPs or on SEND Support.

Some schools also appoint SENCo assistants whose role is often to complete the paper work after EHAT and TAM meetings and after annual reviews. Some settings may appoint SEND teaching assistants who provide the interventions for pupils within the school. These two additions can really support a SENCo in what they are able to do to improve provision for pupils with special educational needs in their school.

A SENCo has often been a subject leader within a school and is looking for the next stage of progression. It could be that the member of staff does not yet want the responsibility of a deputy or assistant head or that this is something that does not appeal to them. The role of the SENCo is whole school and should be part of the senior leadership team (either formally or informally), making strategic change across the school. For some settings, the head or deputy/assistant head may have the SENCo responsibility. In taking the role, the SENCo commits to completing a postgraduate qualification or NPQ paid for by the school. This is a valuable professional opportunity which not many teachers have.

SENCos will often take the lead in terms of pastoral support within the school. Child protection may also be an addition to the role, however this can blur lines with families you may have worked hard to support and can damage relationships if not managed appropriately. Therefore, this model is not always recommended.

The role is varied and fast paced. With skill and humour, you can manage your own diary and that is often something teachers appreciate when moving into the post.

In this role you get to witness progress at first hand. By planning and deploying staff to deliver interventions, pupils can progress in small steps. Progress measured may not be towards academic goals. Often interventions for SEND can be linked to behaviour, social skills or life skills and this can be a welcome break for a teacher who has been consumed with attainment.

Further, and importantly for your organisation, you get to build relationships with many different stakeholders. There is the essential responsibility of line managing teaching assistants or pastoral staff. There is a chance to work closely with parents and be actively involved in supporting families. You will also lead on creating plans with professionals from external agencies to improve the opportunities available to pupils with SEND.

The role of a SENCo may afford opportunities for creative thinking and strategic planning. By joining working parties, trialling different practices and feeding back at a local level within a partnership of schools, a SENCo can bring about systemic change within their organisation.

By common consent across the nation's staffrooms, this is a challenging and exciting role, especially for someone who is passionate about making positive change for *all* pupils. The system – today and tomorrow – needs more teachers willing to step up to lead special educational needs.

ASIDE

Is the role of SENCo for everyone?

Some teachers/headteachers can be allocated the role of SENCo without much choice or say. This is particularly evident in small schools. It can be a challenging role, especially if you do not have much experience of working with pupils with SEND.

Other staff can expect you to be an expert and have answers, perhaps more than in other coordinator roles.

It is also a role that is organic and can frequently change as children join and leave your school and cohorts change.

We have always felt that it is best to follow the interest and knowledge of your teachers when allocating leadership roles and the SENCo role is no exception.

- Why are you a SENCo?
- Why do you want to become one?
- Why would you recommend the role to others (or not)?
- What are your strengths as a teacher that would particularly lend themselves to you becoming a successful SEND leader?
- How would others describe your practices with regard to pupils with special needs?

Test yourself against Ofsted!

Here are two recommendation paragraphs – similarly worded – from Ofsted reports of schools rated as 'Good'. Reflecting on their critique, could Ofsted write these paragraphs about your school? You will argue *no*, because of the successful work you do!

'Some staff are not always adapting the curriculum well enough to meet the needs of pupils with SEND. Consequently, some pupils with SEND do not achieve sufficiently well. Leaders should ensure that staff receive appropriate training to adapt the curriculum to meet the needs of pupils with SEND so that they are supported to do as well as they can.'

'Teachers do not always adapt learning for pupils with SEND clearly enough. This means that some of these pupils do not achieve as well as they could. The school, with support from the trust, should provide the training and resources teachers need to adapt the learning and support all pupils with SEND more effectively.'

(Source: Crown Copyright)[3]

---

3   Material from Ofsted reports reproduced with permission: Crown Copyright.

ZONES

ZONES OF PROXIMAL DEVELOPMENT (VYGOTSKY, 1978)

When training to be a teacher and considering how children learn, Vygotsky's notion of 'zones of proximal development' (1978) is often referenced. Vygotsky believed that in order for children to progress, they need to be set activities which are just out of their academic reach if completed independently. If an adult or able peer supports at this point with scaffolding, positive social interaction and encouragement, the child is more likely to achieve.

In order to do this, staff need to be aware of what a pupil does know through methods of assessment for learning. The zone of proximal development is an organic process that shifts as new skills are achieved.

You may well need to support school staff to understand what the zone of proximal development looks like for different pupils with SEND. Learning walks and observations will allow you to ascertain whether pupils are being taught appropriately and to determine whether assessments are accurate. Pupils with more significant needs may work with teaching assistants, therefore it would be important for the TAs to be aware of this theory and how it can support the pupils they are working with.

Teachers are often reluctant to use this approach for pupils with SEN, whether this is a lack of confidence in how best to scaffold learning for a particular need that a pupil may have or not wanting risk the possibility that it may harm a child's self-esteem or lead to them being dysregulated. This is completely understandable, but it is the SENCo's role to identify where this is happening and then support the teacher or other adult working with that child to be as ambitious as they can.

ZONES OF REGULATION (KUYPERS, 2023)

When considering supporting pupils with their emotional literacy and SEMH need, Zones of Regulation is a resource that has become more popular in schools across the globe in supporting self-regulation. This resource can be taught independently, as a group, with an individual class or, in some cases, with a whole school. When using the resource for a whole class or school, a universal language develops that children can use to discuss how they are feeling.

Emotions are linked to four colours (blue, green, yellow and red). These colours can be displayed in classrooms to help children identify how they are feeling and what strategies they can use to support themselves. Staff members can also have small versions of this resource which they can wear on their lanyards to support pupils when moving around the school. This approach can be very successful and supports children, especially those with speech and language challenges, that may struggle to find words that describe how they are feeling.

Where it works best is when staff also adopt this approach and use the same language when talking to children about how they are feeling. Children are taught about brain science and what happens to us when we dysregulate.

It may be your role to implement a new resource such as the Zones of Regulation. You could be tasked with creating an action plan to introduce the new resource and train staff. You may need to decide whether some pupils need additional small-group or 1:1 work which could be part of an IEP and recorded on the provision map.

If you have completed the implementation stage, it would also be your role to evaluate its impact. This could be done by collecting SEMH/wellbeing questionnaires, pupil/staff voice or monitoring the number of sanctions across the school regarding challenging behaviour linked to dysregulation.

As with any new initiative, it is always wise to share with parents. This can be done briefly through newsletters or information on the school website. A parent event, where ideas can be shared and suggestions of how parents can use this in the family home, will consolidate the learning that is happening at school and aid the progress of the child. It can also be beneficial to share resources with parents that they can use at home, if this is affordable; if it is not, consider what financial support the school might be able to offer.

ZONES WITHIN THE CLASSROOM

When teachers are developing their learning environment, it is important that they consider all the pupils in their class. Children respond to routine and part of the school experience is to help them to develop their independence. Having set zones within the classroom, for English resources or displays and maths resources, for example, will support children's self-help skills. Resources should be labelled so that children can easily find what they are looking for. Photographs of the resource or symbols could be used to support those children who are unable to read, particularly those with special educational needs.

Classrooms can be over-stimulating for some children and so it may be worthwhile to create some quieter 'zones' within the classroom. This could include a book nook with cushions, story books and blankets. Another useful zone could be a sensory corner with a tent or teepee, or just a blanket over a table, where children can retreat to if they are feeling over-stimulated or overwhelmed. Some children may benefit from having a card or symbol that they can show if they feel they need some time out of the classroom to support regulation. (Timers would also support this transition.)

ZONES WITHIN THE SCHOOL

As with the classroom, it will support pupils if the layout of the school and use of certain rooms does not change. It can also be helpful to have zones within the school where children know they can receive support or quieter zones that are available if necessary. Signs and symbols should also be used to make the school as inclusive as possible.

As with the inside of a school, the playground and outside space can also be zoned to support pupils. There can be an area where children can seek support or find a friend if feeling lonely. Some schools offer peer support on the playground by training particular children in games, conflict resolution and how to help other children who may be struggling socially. There may also be an area where children can develop their gross motor skills with climbing equipment or an area where there are chalks for drawing and writing.

THE IMPORTANCE OF GREEN

What is offered in a playground can often be limited by where the school is. Inner-city schools have little opportunity to offer green space, while schools in the suburbs and in the countryside may have more versatile grounds.

Research has shown that access to green space can support children to regulate, develop academically and can improve their health.

An area of the playground could be dedicated to growing plants and flowers in raised beds. Although this may not be as beneficial as acres of green grass, it can offer something additional and teach children something new. By carefully considering what is planted, you can link the area to different curriculum subjects throughout the year: measuring the height of sunflowers in maths, labelling plants in science or sketching flowers in art. The senses can also be stimulated by growing plants with strong scents, such as lavender. Children can also observe the wildlife that is attracted to the raised beds.

The development and growth of the area can form part of an after-school group or intervention. Involving parents in this resource is a good way of sharing knowledge. You may have a parent who is an avid gardener who can help and make suggestions, or the work that is happening at school may encourage parents to try something similar in the family home.

It is important to get children used to the different areas within a school when there are transitions between year groups.

ASIDE

It can be easy to end up stuck in your office completing paperwork, or in virtual meetings. Although this is important and something that can often feel unavoidable, what is the most important work a SENCo does and in which 'zone' does that work take place? What do you reflect when you read these points?

- Most SENCos will share that they wish they could do more direct work with pupils.

- Leaders can comment that they wish SENCos could spend more time supporting teachers with their inclusive practice in the classroom.

- Parents can share that they want the SENCo to prioritise finding external, specialist support to help their child achieve.

The authors conclude that a variety of this work, carefully planned and reflecting whole-school priorities, is the 'Golden Ticket'.

SECTION
TWO

THE VOICE OF A SENCO

'Unity, not uniformity, must be our aim. We attain unity only through variety. Differences must be integrated, not annihilated, not absorbed.'

Mary Parker Follett

This first part of Section Two – referred to in parts of Section One – brings together the collective SENCo experience of well over 100 years, providing support, advice and general tips from various settings, including primary, secondary, special and alternative provision, as well as inner city, rural and coastal schools.

By way of research for the book, we interviewed ten SENCos; some interviews were face-to-face while others were virtual. They were all very busy people and equally keen to share their experiences with us.

Every school has a statutory duty to have a SENCo, all of whom face similar challenges and barriers and often requiring the same solutions, so you would expect a collective approach to many of these areas. Yet all too often, SENCos operate in isolation, and it can be quite a lonely role. In our work, we always advocate for connecting with others, locally or nationally, including using the potential of social media.

Without exception, all SENCos have a strong moral purpose in their role. While they have had different motivations and journeys into the position, they consistently put the child at the centre of their thinking and each and every decision they make. Collectively, one of the biggest frustrations was not being able to do everything they could for the child, whether due to funding issues, time, other resource constraints, or a lack of experience or expertise in a particular area.

Being in a multi-academy trust can be helpful, as there will be a group of SENCos on tap who will share a common purpose and common values, as well as a consistent set of systems and processes. One of our interviewees, a primary colleague who was part of a medium-sized MAT, took it on herself to contact all the SENCos in her trust and arranged an online meeting. Initially, this was a very informal gathering, but very cathartic for all those who attended. It quickly became a forum to share best practice and ways of working and has resulted in some common systems that all the schools in the trust use, thereby making everyone more efficient and effective. For larger trusts, there is often a trust-wide role for SEND or inclusion. For those schools that have this layer, it can be a really helpful sounding board and source of advice.

If you have these forums, try being an active participant. It sometimes feels as though you don't have time, but experience would suggest that it can pay dividends.

FIVE TOP TIPS ARISING FROM THE INTERVIEWS
1. Try not to do everything yourself

If it has not already become apparent, time will soon emerge as your most valuable commodity. Anything you can do to enable yourself to be most effective with it will be paramount. One of these things is ensuring that other staff fulfil their roles and responsibilities. While our natural inclination is to do things for people, it is crucial not to fall into the trap of being all things to all people. It simply won't work!

A constant frustration is that SENCos are often overlooked for any leadership training the school provides – most training for SENCos is in special needs. It is a whole-school leadership role and should be viewed as such. Many colleagues shared this frustration and felt that they were put in a role where they were suddenly line managing a group of teaching assistants as well as trying to champion and raise the profile of SEND across the school. No easy task.

If you can, try to attend any leadership training that any of the subject leaders attend, including some of the National Professional Qualifications (NPQs). One of the SENCos interviewed was currently undertaking the NPQSL (the NPQ in Senior Leadership). They found the process of completing the NPQ particularly beneficial to developing their school leadership, but also benefited from meeting and working with other school leaders in different roles and contexts.

The realisation that it is not possible to do everything may only happen after becoming overwhelmed with everything or after a couple of years in the role. An aspect highlighted by a secondary SENCo was the importance of getting teaching staff on board and understanding their responsibilities. This needs to be clear and done in a way that is supportive and collaborative.

Some staff will need more support than others, and there is a skill in identifying who needs it the most. Ultimately, getting this right will not only save you time but will also free you up to focus on work that only you can and should do. While this won't happen immediately, all the SENCos expressed frustration at the time it took, it is important to acknowledge that perfection in this area is elusive.

One primary colleague emphasised that it is the classroom teacher who knows the pupils the most, making them best placed to provide the level of support and feedback on what is and is not working. Strong links with class teachers/tutors are thus vital.

2. Leading and managing teaching assistants

An important group of staff, which may vary depending on the school's size and structure, are the teaching assistants (TAs). They are an incredible but often underutilised resource in many schools. Many SENCos quickly pointed out that it should be a priority to get to know your TAs as soon as possible and learn about their areas of expertise. By understanding the strengths of your TAs and getting to know them better, you will be able to delegate roles appropriately.

There were a number of variations in how interviewees deployed their colleagues. It is no surprise that the majority of the time, TAs are in class supporting individuals or small groups of pupils. A secondary SENCo stated that she has learned the hard way the importance of knowing her TAs well: knowing who works best with certain types of pupils, who is better at managing behaviour, who is better at working with pupils with gaps in their literacy, for example.

It is not always easy to do this and just relying on what the TAs think their strengths are is not always appropriate. One of the SENCOs from a large primary school suggested that her TAs have a period of their timetable set aside every week to create or differentiate/adapt resources for teachers. There are two notable benefits to this. Firstly, this allows some non-contact time for staff that are often at the forefront of supporting the most challenging children. Secondly, this helps the teachers provide a much higher level of support and curriculum adaptions in their lessons.

3. Planning your diary

If, like most SENCos, you were recently a classroom teacher – either part time or full time – you would have had very little autonomy over your day. This changes suddenly as a SENCo; many of those interviewed said it takes some adjustment and practice to make the best use of your time.

A good piece of advice is to try to compartmentalise your days and weeks, allocating a specific period per week for meeting with parents, depending on the days you work and how much non-contact time you have. If the office staff are aware of this, then, when a parent gets in contact, barring an emergency, they know to book them in this allocated time. This provides reassurance that you won't be disturbed and allows you to plan for any meeting with parents, obtaining necessary information beforehand.

This can extend to other areas of your work: can you allocate time for lesson monitoring, EHCP reviews, interviewing children, looking at resources? Meetings with outside agencies may be less controllable, but you can plan for these if you are strict with yourself – and others!

The life of a SENCo often feels like a series of meetings; with the increase in video calling, this has been made easier but often results in more meetings. Everyone interviewed emphasised the importance of planning and preparing for meetings. If you are attending a meeting, review the agenda; which items should you contribute to, what information might you need? Additionally, unless this is the first meeting, review the actions assigned to you from previous meetings. Be prepared to give an update on these. If they haven't been completed, outline reasons why.

Almost all interviewees described a time when they attended a meeting unprepared, and the feeling of being exposed – something they only wanted to experience once!

One surprising element many colleagues were unprepared for was the expectation of chairing meetings. This is something that you do not receive training for and it can be quite challenging and daunting. The key here is being prepared and taking time to plan for these meetings, obtaining agendas and any paperwork in advance. (See 5 below.)

4. Developing relationships

Relationships with parents

This comes top of the list as perhaps the most challenging to get right. It is the most fraught with pitfalls but, if done right, can be the most beneficial.

The advice from many of the interviews was not to be afraid to be honest with parents. Sometimes difficult messages need to be delivered and this can be a cause for anxiety, but, ultimately, parents want to know and will appreciate this in the long run, even though it may not always feel like it.

A collection of tips on managing parents:

- Check what form of communication is best for the parent. It might be by phone, email or face to face.

- Keep parents central to the process. Talk to them before changing provision, routine and support. It does not mean you are necessarily asking their permission, but seeking views and pre-warning them of changes is really important.

- If you say you are going to do something, then make sure you do it. Sometimes this is also about managing expectations. Do not over-promise; give realistic timescales of when things may be completed.

- Admit mistakes. We all make mistakes and get things wrong sometimes; there is no shame in letting parents know if you haven't got things right. Just tell them as soon as possible and let them know what you are going to do to rectify it.

- Be passionate and knowledgeable. (And if you do not know something, aim to find out.) Parents want to see that you care. They may have fought to get their child the support they need and, quite often, the SENCo is their only advocate in the school.

Relationships with staff

Managing up, down and sideways! What do we mean by this? Many interviewees talked about feeling that they were caught in the middle at times. They often have to spend a lot of time trying to influence other teachers and teaching assistants as well as other subject and pastoral leaders. One area that we did not expect to come up so strongly in our discussions with SENCos was about the challenges they have had with other senior leaders in their schools.

We would not expect any headteacher or other member of a senior leadership team not to value or rate the importance of supporting pupils with SEND in a school, but with so many competing priorities for time, resources and the high-stakes accountability, it can seem that way at times. It can often take bravery to advocate for a certain child, for a specific provision or for a way of doing things with people more senior to you, but this is what you may have to do.

Relationships with local authorities

Getting to know the key people in your local authority (LA) is vital. This can feel like an uphill battle at times as there are often multiple people that you have to engage with and their roles and responsibilities tend to change frequently. It is no secret that many LAs are under increasing financial pressure which may mean there are more staff changes and it can often feel like an adversarial relationship.

One experienced colleague recommends that you attend as many LA SEND events, training, workshops and briefings as your diary allows. Your face will soon become recognised and the LA officers will appreciate your engagement. Although it does not always feel like it, they want what is best for the child as well, so an appreciation of their restraints and issues goes a long way.

Relationships with other agencies

There will be many other agencies that may want to work with you or pupils in your school or that are required to provide advice or direct support. As with everything, the advice from the SENCos interviewed is: use your judgement on what you feel is right for the child, and talk it through with a colleague if something doesn't feel right.

5. Chairing meetings

Outlined below is a summary of the advice shared about how to run a successful meeting.

Be prepared:

- Familiarise yourself with the agenda and any relevant documents beforehand.
- Anticipate potential issues and prepare solutions or strategies to address them.

Set clear objectives:

- Clearly articulate the purpose of the meeting and the specific outcomes you hope to achieve.
- Share the agenda in advance so that participants can come prepared.

Create a positive atmosphere:

- Foster an inclusive and supportive environment where everyone feels comfortable sharing their perspectives.

Establish ground rules:

- Set expectations for behaviour (phones on silent!), such as listening respectfully, allowing everyone to speak and staying focused on the agenda. (This one is context dependent and generally only applies to the first meeting together.) Virtual meetings and recordings of meetings also need ground rules.
- Encourage active participation and ensure that all voices are heard but remain in control of the meeting.

Use effective communication:

- Articulate your points clearly and facilitate discussions to ensure that information is understood.
- Encourage open communication and be receptive to feedback and suggestions.

Manage time effectively:

- Start and end the meeting on time to respect participants' schedules.
- Allocate specific time slots for each agenda item and stick to the schedule.

Encourage collaboration:

- Facilitate collaborative problem-solving and decision-making.
- Ensure that team members feel their input is valued and that they play an active role in the decision-making process.

Document actions and decisions:

- Keep accurate minutes of the meeting, including key points discussed, decisions made and action items assigned. (Try to get someone reliable to do this. It is difficult to chair and minute the meetings at the same time.)
- Share the minutes promptly after the meeting to reinforce accountability.

Seek feedback:

- Encourage participants to provide feedback on the meetings, including what worked well and areas for improvement.
- Use feedback to refine your approach and make future meetings more effective.

Remember that effective meeting leadership is a skill that develops over time. Be open to learning from each experience and continuously strive to improve your chairing abilities. Nearly all the SENCos commented that even after many years, they still often found this aspect difficult and are always looking to improve. They also said that it can be helpful to reflect on meetings that you aren't chairing and look for how others do it, both positive and negative elements.

With the authors' warm acknowledgements to colleagues who gave up their time to be interviewed.

RESOURCES FOR PROFESSIONAL DEVELOPMENT

1. INCLUSIVE TEACHING OBSERVATION CHECKLIST

	Yes/No	Evidence
Has the teacher identified differentiated learning goals for those working significantly below their peers and adapted learning to ensure all can reach the learning outcome?		
Is there use of multi-sensory teaching approaches and/or approaches that enable some students to use more concrete learning aids?		
Is there use of interactive strategies, e.g. students being invited to come to the front to take a role, or having their own whiteboards to support their learning?		
Is there use of visual and tangible aids for all students: real objects, signs or symbols, photographs etc.?		
Does the teacher find ways of making abstract concepts concrete, e.g. using pictures to illustrate word problems in maths, modelling with concrete resources?		
Does the teacher use both simplified tasks for some groups (e.g. with shorter concrete texts) and extended, more-abstract tasks for others?		
Are tasks made 'closed' or more 'open' to suit students' current learning needs?		
Over time, does the teacher employ a variety of pupil groupings?		

	Yes/No	Evidence
Can all students hear/see the teacher clearly, and any resources in use?		
Is new or difficult vocabulary discussed and clarified, displayed and returned to?		
Does the teacher check for understanding of concepts?		
Does the teacher ask students to explain instructions in their own words?		
Are questions pitched to challenge pupils at all levels?		
Is this a secure and supportive learning environment where there is safety to have a go and make mistakes?		
Does the teacher give personal thinking time before responses are required? Is progressively more scaffolding offered until a student can answer correctly?		
Is extra adult support for lower-achieving students used in ways that promote autonomy, encourage self-esteem and increase students' inclusion within the group?		
Do the adults who provide extra support in the classroom clearly know what the students are to learn?		
Does the teacher work directly with lower-attaining groups as well as the more able?		
Does the teacher explain, or model, tasks clearly? Does he/she check students have understood what they have to do?		
Are pupils provided with, and reminded of, resources to help them be autonomous (e.g. word lists or mats, dictionaries of terms, glossaries, number lines, tables squares)?		
Does the teacher use scaffolding (e.g. writing frames) to support learners to complete the required activities?		

	Yes/No	Evidence
Has the teacher made arrangements, where necessary, to ensure that all students have access to all written texts?		
Has the teacher planned alternatives to written tasks, where appropriate?		
Does the teacher make effective use of ICT as an access strategy for some students where appropriate?		
Is desired behaviour noticed and praised, rewarded or encouraged?		
Are all students involved in setting their own targets and monitoring their own progress?		

2. KEY TASKS FOR THE YEAR

Item	Task	Completed
SENCo planner for the year	• Ensure you have an annual planner for the management of SEND with key tasks that need to be completed throughout the year.	
Action plan for the year	• Collect and analyse SEND data from previous year. • Identify key areas for development and include in a SEND action plan. • Consider what staff CPD opportunities are needed such as understanding of the Code of Practice, High Quality Teaching.	
Statutory documents for published SEND information relating to your school	• Look at your school website and ensure the following documents are on it and up to date: SEND Information Report, SEND Policy, Accessibility Plan. • Review annually and ensure parents, carers and CYP (children and young people) are involved in the review of policies and the SEND Information Report.	
SEND list	• Locate most recent SEND list/register. • Update to include: • pupil name/DOB/year group/class • need type • level of SEND: SEND Support/EHCP/Under assessment. (You may want to highlight which SEND Support pupils have additional high-needs funding.) • You may want to have an additional list of pupils who are not currently SEND Support but are vulnerable or a cause for concern based on information from pupil progress meetings and/or from school tracking systems.	

Item	Task	Completed
SEND funding	• Ensure you understand the amount of notional SEND budget allocated to your school and the amount of Top-Up funding allocated for pupils with an EHCP. • Ensure you know: • how this funding is spent • whether it is value for money • whether it impacts on outcomes.	
Planning EHCP annual reviews	At the start of the autumn term, make a list of all pupils with SEND requiring an annual review (all pupils with an EHCP).	
Planning provision	• Locate most recent whole-school provision map. • Review whole-school provision map based on current needs of pupils across the school. • Co-production of the whole-school provision map with teachers, SENCo, parents and senior teachers is recommended. • Plan whole-school SEND provision for the current academic year, including frequency, cost and measurable outcomes. • Plan individual pupil provision for SEND Support pupils. • Ensure you have in place systems for monitoring provision and ways to measure impact. This should be based on an assess-plan-do-review cycle. • Identify training needs and TA deployment.	
Monitoring	• Plan a monitoring timetable for the year to include the following: • lesson/intervention observations • termly learning walks • planning and work scrutiny • high-quality teaching audit • termly SEND data analysis • participation in pupil progress meetings.	

Item	Task	Completed
Liaison with SEND governor and full governing body	• Find out who the SEND governor is and make contact with them. • Invite them to meetings that involve them in co-production such as SEND audit, review of policies etc. • Share action plan for the year and key priorities. • Arrange update meetings with SEND governor each term. Minute and record meetings. • Consider SEND governor joining you on a SEND learning walk. • Write end-of-year SEND report for governors.	

3. INDIVIDUAL BEHAVIOUR PLAN

(Examples in italic)

Name		Date		Version	
		Date of birth		SEND stage	

Behaviours witnessed	Staff approach
Stage 1	
Chewing on jumper	*Offer a job*
Hiding	*Quiet conversation*
Clinging to parents	*Story*
Stage 2	
Shouting	*'I can see you are angry. Let's tidy this up then we can . . .'*
Throwing resources	
	'I wonder if . . .'
Stage 3	
Biting adults	*Clear children from space*
Hitting children	*Physical intervention if necessary*
Stage 4	
Crying	*Offer drink*
Hiding	*Story*
Hot	*Quiet time with trusted adult*

Notification (copy of the plan to ...)

SLT   SENCo   Parents/Guardians

Relevant staff

Names: ....

Review date: ....

4. REFLECTION SHEET

Name: ....

Date: ....

I feel:
Colour or draw

I was not ready, respectful, safe because:

Next time, to avoid a sanction I should:

5. SEND CHILD REVIEW

This form is an easy way to record conversations and track progress of those trickier cases. Best practice would be for the SENCo to meet 3× a year with class teachers to discuss pupils with SEND or any pupils who may be causing concern.

Year group	Child	Provision: Summer	Provision: Autumn	Provision: Spring	Provision: Summer

6. SUPPORT PLAN
(examples in italics)

Student name	DOB	Year group	Tutor group	Date reviewed	SEND stage

SEND needs

ASD

ADHD

Epilepsy, dyslexia & dyspraxia

Strengths & interests	Weaknesses & difficulties
• *Playing with friends and family* • *Dodgeball* • *Football* • *Basketball* • *Xbox*	• *Student missed a year of education* • *Struggles to read and write* • *Handwriting is illegible* • *No organisation skills – please check regularly that he has his everyday things with him* • *Please keep a watchful eye on student – he will not say if he is being bullied* • *Struggles to make friends*
Quality First Teaching (QTF) provision	**Additional To/Different From (ATDF) provision**
• *Repeat clear and concise instructions* • *Don't raise voice* • *Use of name* • *Make sure you have his attention when giving instructions* • *Do not ask to read aloud* • *Highlight essential information* • *Scaffolding e.g. a task ladder or now/next* • *Movement breaks* • *Help with recording his work* • *Visual cues* • *Repetition and practice of key knowledge* • *Encourage 'why' questions* • *Minimise distractions* • *Model conversations*	• *Doodle book/paper to draw on during rest breaks* • *Rest breaks* • *Prompter* • *TA Support* • *Key worker* • *Lego club/crafts club* • *Social games/stories* • *No nonsense phonics* • *Learning support – external agency* • *Visual timetable* • *Fidget toy*

Intervention	Target
Flying high – handwriting	*Improve handwriting so 5 minutes of written work is legible by XXXX*
Social games/social stories	*Student will have appropriate conversations with one peer during unstructured time 4 out of 5 times by XXXX*
	Student will recognise a 'big feeling' and identify one trigger for this 3 out of 5 times by XXXX
No nonsense phonics	*To gain sounds 'ur' 'ce' and 'cy' by XXXX*
	Secure missing phonics sounds from books 8 and 9 by XXXX (see phonics tracker)
	Student will have increased the number of legible words in a piece of independent writing by XXXX
Lego/craft club	*Student will express himself freely during Lego or craft club 4 out of 5 times by April 2024*
	Student will use eye contact with a similar-aged peer and an adult in Lego/craft clubs 4 out of 5 times by XXXX
Learning support – external agency	*Student will complete his maths b-squared targets on calculation by April 2024*
Classroom strategies and TA support	*Student will recall a piece of information from present learning during plenary by XXXX*
	Student will be able to focus for up to 5 minutes on independent work by XXXX
	Student will ask a question to his TA or teacher daily 4 out of 5 times by XXXX
	Student will understand a two-step instruction, 2 out of 5 times by XXXX
	Student will use his movement to help regulate his emotions 5 out of 5 times by XXXX
	Student will be able to recognise when he needs a movement break to regulate his emotions 3 out 5 times by XXXX

Triggers	Access arrangements
• *Not understanding the work* • *Making friends*	
Additional information	

7. INDIVIDUAL EDUCATION PLAN TEMPLATE

IEP start date: IEP review date:

Areas to be developed	SMART Target	Strategies/Provision/ Intervention (additional to/different from)	Key staff, where and when	Progress made towards target	Achieved RAG

Things I want you to know about me:	It would help me if you could:
My strengths are:	I will help myself by:
I find it challenging to:	To help me learn at home, my family will:

We discussed this plan …

Parent signature	Child signature	School signature

Parent comment

Child comment

8. WHOLE-SCHOOL PROVISION PLANNING

Intervention	Targeted pupils	Cost	Duration	Short term outcomes (include qualitative and quantitative measures)

9. INTERVENTION NOTES

Intervention title:

Date	Attendees (initials)	Notes (what was planned)	AFL	Next steps

10. INDIVIDUAL PROVISION MAP

(examples in italics)

Intervention	Target – Term 1	Target – Term 2	Target – Term 3	EHCP outcome
Sensory diet	*Be able to independently complete his sensory diet 3 out of 5 times by December 2024*			
RWI – phonics	*Be able to recognise sounds 'ch', 't' and 'at' by December 2024*			
Universal SLT provision	*For Dami to stay focused on a task with adult support for 5 minutes, 3 out of 5 times by December 2024*			
Universal OT provision	*Be able to sit on his chair for 10 minutes, 3 out of 5 times by December 2024*			
SLT 1on1	*To be able to subcategorise semantic categories food, animals, transport and clothes with 90% accuracy by December 2024*			
Meet 'n' greet	*Start period 1 'green' 3 out of 5 times by December 2024*			

Intervention	Target – Term 1	Target – Term 2	Target – Term 3	EHCP outcome
SLT colourful semantics group	To be able to build subject-verb-object (SVO) sentences from picture stimuli with 50% accuracy by December 2024			
SLT phonological awareness	Dami will be able to substitute the first sound in words with 80% accuracy by December 2024			

GLOSSARY

CAMHS – Child and Adolescent Mental Health Service

Co-production – Created with a variety of stakeholders including parents, pupil, school staff and external agencies

DfE – Department for Education (UK)

EAL – English as an additional language

ECT – Early career teacher

EEF – Education Endowment Foundation

EHAT – Early Help Assessment Tool

EHCP – Education, Health and Care Plan

EBSA – Emotionally based school avoidance

ESFA – Education and Skills Funding Agency

FOI – Freedom of Information request

IEP – Individual Education Plan

LA – Local authority

LEA – Local education authority (historic)

MAT – Multi-academy trust

NASEN – National Association for Special Educational Needs

NASENCo – National Award for Special Educational Needs Coordination

NPQs – National Professional Qualifications

PA – Persistent absence: less than 90% attendance

PAN – Planned admission number

SA – Severely absent: less than 50% attendance

SAR – Subject access request

SEMH – Social, emotional and mental health

SEND – Special educational needs and disabilities

SENDIASS – Special Educational Needs and Disabilities Information Advice and Support Service

SLT – Senior leadership team

SMART – Specific, measurable, achievable, relevant and time-bound (targets)

SPD – Sensory Processing Disorder

SSP – Systematic Synthetic Phonics

STORM – Skills-based Training on Risk Management

TA – Teaching assistant

TAM – Team Around Me

TISUK – Trauma Informed Schools UK

The A–Z series focuses on the 'fun and fundamentals' of what's happening in primary, special and secondary schools today. Each title is written by a leading practitioner, adopting a series approach of reflection, advice and provocation.

As a group of authors with a strong belief in the power of education to shape and change young people's lives, we hope teachers and leaders in the UK and internationally enjoy what we have to say.

Roy Blatchford, series editor

REFERENCES

Bennett, T. (2020). *Running the Room: The Teacher's Guide to Behaviour.* Woodbridge: John Catt Educational Ltd.

Department for Education. (2011). 'Teachers' Standards'. Available at: https://www.gov.uk/government/publications/teachers-standards

Department for Education. (2019). 'Early career framework'. Available at: https://www.gov.uk/government/publications/early-career-framework

Department for Education. (2024). 'Keeping children safe in education'. Available at: https://www.gov.uk/government/publications/keeping-children-safe-in-education--2

Department for Education and Department of Health and Social Care. (2014). 'SEND Code of Practice: 0 to 25 years'. Available at: https://www.gov.uk/government/publications/send-code-of-practice-0-to-25

Dix, P. (2017). *When the Adults Change, Everything Changes.* Carmarthen: Independent Thinking Press.

Education Endowment Foundation. (2022) 'Moving from "differentiation" to "adaptive teaching".' (a blog). EEF. Available at: https://educationendowmentfoundation.org.uk/news/moving-from-differentiation-to-adaptive-teaching

Florian, L. & Black-Hawkins, K. (2013). 'Exploring inclusive pedagogy'. *British Educational Research Journal.* 37(5), pp. 813–828.

Gatsby Charitable Foundation. (n.d.). The Gatsby Benchmarks of Good Career Guidance. Available at: https://www.gatsby.org.uk/education/focus-areas/good-career-guidance

Gov.uk. (2017). 'Workplace health needs assessment'. Available at: https://www.gov.uk/government/publications/workplace-health-needs-assessment

Gov.uk. (2024) 'Special educational needs in England: Academic year 2023/2024'. Available at: https://explore-education-statistics.service.gov.uk/find-statistics/special-educational-needs-in-england

Kuypers, L.M. (2023). *The Zones of Regulation.* Santa Clara, CA: Think Social Publishing.

Ludlow, R. (2012). *The Little Book of Gross Motor Skills.* Bury: Featherstone.

Maslow, A.H. (1943). 'A theory of human motivation'. *Psychological Review.* 50(4), pp. 370–396. https://doi.org/10.1037/h0054346

NurtureUK. (2023). 'The six principles of nurture'. Available at: https://www.nurtureuk.org/the-six-principles-of-nurture/

Smith, J. (2003). *Activities for Gross Motor Skills Development.* Garden Grove, CA: Teacher Created Resources.

Vygotsky, L.S. (1978). *Mind in Society: The Development of Higher Psychological Processes.* Massachusetts: Harvard University Press.